Triangular Teaching

Triangular Teaching

A New Way of Teaching the Bible to Adults

Barbara A. Bruce

Abingdon Press / Nashville

TRIANGULAR TEACHING
A New Way of Teaching the Bible to Adults

Copyright © 2007 by Abingdon Press

This book is printed on acid-free, elemental chlorine-free paper.

ISBN: 978-0-687-64352-3

06 07 08 09 10 11 12 13 14 15—10 9 8 7 6 5 4 3 2 1

MANUFACTURED IN THE UNITED STATES OF AMERICA

Contents

Preface

I am an educator and will be until the day I die. My passion is "metacognition," that is, learning about learning. I continually pursue new theories and think about how people learn. While some of the content of this book is based on technical research, much of the book contains activities based on my own "learning laboratory"—practices that have been born out of many years of teaching and the wisdom that comes only from trial and error in adult classroom situations.

My first discoveries dealt with what works. I discovered tools and techniques that made learning both fun and formative. That wasn't enough. I had a need to know why. Why did some techniques work better than others? I am finding some right answers. My search for learning about learning continues. I want to know both the how's and the why's of a good teaching and learning experience. The more we know about the how's and why's of excellent teaching, the more we can help people integrate the message of the Bible into their own lives.

My formal background includes a bachelor's degree in education and a master's degree in creative studies. Combining these two areas of my professional life made teaching come to life in countless ways. I began to include creative and critical thinking activities in my teaching even as I was completing my graduate work. Helping people to think beyond their normal activities led to breakthroughs in grasping concepts and in faith development. As my personal studies continued, I discovered the work of Howard Gardner and his disciples. I began to include the concepts of multiple avenues of learning and was able to recognize a cause and effect relationship as to why some teaching/learning sessions were more effective than others. As I continued to purposefully implement these teaching strategies, I saw more positive responses from the learners. Across the country I heard stories of relief and joy as people told me their personal discoveries about how they learn best. Research has clearly demonstrated that we do not all learn the same way and that specific strategies exist that will help teachers and leaders address differences in ways of learning.

Teaching and preaching the concepts of creative and critical thinking and multiple intelligence theory for more than a decade led me to the learning brain. This knowledge added yet another significant layer to my understanding of why certain teaching/leaning techniques work well and the absence of them can make teaching fall on deaf and/or bored ears.

I believe the combination of three major areas of cognitive understanding—creative and critical thinking, multiple intelligences, and knowing something about how the brain learns—can lead to the most exciting, enriching, and exhilarating discoveries when adults apply them to their learning process. This multidisciplinary approach may open and expand even the best teaching/learning process.

My passion for learning about learning has led me on a fantastic journey of discovery. I am in the midst of a continual learning laboratory as I travel around the country working with teachers and leaders. My goal for this book is to place the information gleaned from my learning discoveries in the hands of teachers and leaders of God's people. Good teachers have been incorporating many of these techniques for hundreds, even thousands, of years. While Jesus did not name the methods of his teaching as I do in this book, he was skillful in discerning the needs of people and in presenting his teachings in ways that met their needs. His methods remain powerful for us today as we seek to learn from him through the Bible.

What I am attempting to do in this book is not simply to provide lessons, but to teach you, as teachers and leaders, why the tools and techniques work and how you can apply them to your teaching/learning experiences. Once you discover how your adult learners will be turned on and tuned in to these concepts, you will wonder how you taught without them. I have learned that the key is explaining what you are doing and why. Bring adult participants into the process and ask for feedback. Their participation and ownership guides me in my teaching as it will guide you in yours.

I want to share a quotation that has spoken to me. It is my wish that this book will help you to discover the keys to the treasure chamber of teaching.

> *I long to put the experience of fifty years at once into your young lives, to give you the key of that treasure chamber every gem of which has cost me tears and struggles and prayers, but you must work for these inward treasures yourselves.*[1]
> —Harriet Beecher Stowe

I wish you the joy of discovery and the excitement of learning God's Word in meaningful and enriching ways.

Blessings,
Barbara Bruce

---

[1] From *Between Ourselves: Letters Between Mothers and Daughters 1750–1982*, edited by Karen Payne (Houghton Mifflin Co., 1983).

Introduction

Understanding Triangular Teaching

Welcome to the wonderful and exciting world of metacognition, or learning about learning!

As Christian educators we are aware that:
- biblical illiteracy is increasingly common in our churches
- adults across age levels are hungering for God's Word
- many adult leaders teach in the very same ways they were taught
- the only constant today is change
- the church needs to find more interesting and challenging ways to present God's Word to adults

How do we as teachers and leaders in Christian education address such issues? How can we best engage adult learners with the Bible? Triangular teaching is a multidisciplinary approach that is one right answer to these pressing issues. I believe triangular teaching—an integration of the teaching techniques that emerge from our knowledge of creative and critical thinking, multiple intelligence theory, and brain research—opens doors for teachers and learners.

Often we go through life with a mental *scotoma*. A scotoma is a blind or dark spot in our visual field. We become so used to what we "see" that we miss the hidden details and beauty around us. I believe we develop a mental scotoma that works with biblical study as well. We read Scripture and our former associations blind us to the deeper meaning and wisdom of what lies before us, waiting for our "aha's" and discoveries. My mission for this book is to remove the blind spots and to lead teachers and learners to discoveries of how Scripture speaks to us every day and has the power to transform our lives.

The information about triangular teaching will help you to understand the reasons behind transformational teaching and learning experiences that engage adult learners. When we understand the reasons behind teaching techniques, we can be intentional about how we teach. We will also find that a greater number of our learners will become engaged with the Scriptures. We will discover that we have presented activities and materials in ways that help them "to see" through the mental scotomas about the Bible.

Triangular teaching includes concepts from three different areas of knowledge: multiple intelligence theory, creative and critical thinking skills, and the findings of brain research. 1. *Multiple intelligence theory* tells us that we all learn in different ways. When we use more than one or two intelligences, our learning increases exponentially. 2. *Creative and critical thinking* stimulates learning through novelty and through challenge. Creative thinking involves processes that put things and information together in new ways in order to create something new or to develop a new way of understanding known ideas. Critical thinking involves processes such as recall of information, comparison, contrast, and analysis in order to learn and to make ideas practical and useable. 3. *Brain research* informs us about the physical processes of the brain. We are beginning to know how the brain learns, and when we use this information to the fullest, learning increases. Brain research supports the use of activities that engage multiple intelligences and that engage critical and creative thinking skills.

1. Multiple Intelligence Theory

We know in the world of education that each person is uniquely created by God with different gifts, interests, and abilities. While we acknowledge this as fact, we often overlook it in our "regular" class sessions. In this adventure in Bible study, we recognize and honor each participant's learning profile. Each person is born with the ability to learn through many different intelligences.

In 1983, Dr. Howard Gardner of Harvard University's "Project Zero" published a book called *Frames of Mind: The Theory of Multiple Intelligences* (Basic Books), which rocked the world of teaching and learning. In it, Gardner outlines the research gleaned from his worldwide study of how people learn. Succinctly, his research states that we are created with at least seven different intelligences. He outlines the possibility of several more in his later books. Essentially, Gardner's theory states that although we are born with many ways of knowing, each of us has learning preferences, and they are different. When educators present information that engages only two or three of these preferences, we diminish the learning capacity of many students. We need to include all of the various ways of knowing in order to meet the needs of a greater number of learners. Both the theory and application of Gardner's theory is presented in *7 Ways of Teaching the Bible to Adults* (Abingdon Press, 2000).

The following is a brief outline of the intelligences:

If your student's preference for learning is . . .

Verbal/Linguistic: Reading, writing, speaking
Include:
creative writing, poetry, debate, storytelling, jokes/limericks, vocabulary, journaling, discussion

Triangular Teaching

Logical/Mathematical: Problem-solving, sequencing, ordering
Include:
abstract symbols, outlining, numbers sequence, syllogisms, pattern discernment, calculations, deciphering codes, cataloging

Visual/Spatial: Looking at charts, pictures, objects; drawing
Include:
guided imagery, mind mapping, costumes, sculpture, active imagination, color schemes, designing, painting

Bodily/Kinesthetic: Manipulating objects, moving the body
Include:
physical exercise, mime, role playing, manipulating objects, body language, drama, physical gestures, charades

Musical/Rhythmic: Tapping rhythms, singing, connecting with music
Include:
musical performance, humming, musical composition, sounds, new words to songs, vibrations, rhythmic patterns, vocal tones

Interpersonal: Working with partners or groups, interacting
Include:
giving feedback, group projects, person-to-person communication, division of labor, collaborating, cooperative learning projects

Intrapersonal: Working alone, reflecting
Include:
silent reflection, know thyself, guided imagery, journaling, emotional processing, metacognition, focusing skills, centering

Naturalist: Using the natural world as a learning tool

Include:
relief maps, caring for God's creatures, habits/habitats of animals/birds, migration patterns, natural surroundings, plants

In Bible study, we can immediately see the application of these ways of learning. Some people love to play with words and need to understand the foundations and backgrounds of Greek and Hebrew words in the Bible (Verbal/Linguistic). Others need to know the history and background information of the particular Bible passage and how it fits together in the overall picture (Logical/Mathematical). There are people whose learning is greatly enhanced when they can see an image or a map or a video clip (Visual/Spatial). Many people will relate to a faith experience through a hymn or song based on a particular Scripture passage (Musical/Rhythmic). Others need to touch such things as grains, stones, or other objects mentioned in Bible stories or to move around the room in order to emulate a biblical journey like the Exodus (Bodily/Kinesthetic). Some learners benefit from discussing a Bible passage with others (Interpersonal), while others prefer to think and reflect quietly either before or instead of sharing thoughts about the passage (Intrapersonal). Some people can relate to Scripture best when it deals with God's creation and the natural world (Naturalist).

Bible study experience that incorporates multiple intelligence theory honors each person's preferred ways of learning. It also encourages testing different approaches and discovering other ways of learning as we explore God's Word for us in this time and place. This theory has become so ingrained in our teaching and learning practices that we often take it for granted. We need to take the time to honor and explore each intelligence. The first lesson, a training lesson for triangular teaching, will help you consider your class profile and to determine which ways of learning are predominate in your group. You may want to create a chart as you plan. When using multiple intelligence theory in a Bible study setting, you not only will include different ways that people learn, you will also invite participants to stretch their learning potential and explore Scripture in new ways.

2. Creative and Critical Thinking

Not only do we all learn differently, but we are created to be co-creators with God. We have been given by our Creator the ability to think both creatively and critically about our world. Imagine a seesaw on a playground. Sometimes one side is up and the other down, but both sides work together to create optimal movement. Likewise, creative and critical thinking are two aspects of the "dynamic balance" of the creative thought process, sometimes creative thinking is up, other times critical thinking is up, but both aspects of the process are necessary for comprehensive learning.

Creative thinking involves:
• making new connections
• thinking and experiencing in many and various ways
• testing different points of view
• considering different possibilities

Critical thinking involves:
• comparing and contrasting ideas
• analyzing and developing possibilities
• screening, selecting, and supporting ideas
• making effective decisions and judgments based on gathered information

The intentional inclusion of both creative and critical thinking skills can open our hearts and minds to new, faith-building ways of examining our understanding of Scripture. The inclusion of critical and creative thinking strategies emulates and builds upon the teaching tools that Jesus used in his teaching. Jesus addressed people where they were, he used familiar objects, he told stories and asked questions. Jesus knew and used the power of metaphor and analogy. All of these and more are tools that stimulate and enhance both creative and critical thinking. Jesus constantly used these tools in teaching the people of his day to understand God's Word. We incorporate those same tools and techniques for our greater understanding of God's Word.

3. Brain Research

Brain research has taught us that learning is dependent upon a combination of physiology and the way you consciously direct your brain's focus and attention. We know that for learning to be complete, it must engage both hemispheres of the brain. To be very succinct, the left hemisphere deals mainly with cognitive, objective, and rational thinking, while the right hemisphere deals with the creative and imaginative aspects of learning. That statement is oversimplified but contains more than a grain of truth. What we do know absolutely is that, in order for the most optimum learning to occur, both hemispheres must be engaged. The exercises contained in this book intentionally include activities that address both hemispheres in the learning of Scripture.

We know from research of the learning brain that when neural pathways are created, they must be sustained. Your brain stores information as a pattern of neurons; and the stronger the pattern, the more lasting the memory. Repetition is critical as the neural pathways are strengthened with continued use. A tool in this experience is to explore what is already known about a concept. This exercise activates the neural pathway by searching for what is already stored. The exercise also brings to light misinformation which can interfere with learning if your brain cannot create meaning. We know that when the brain feels "threatened," it does not operate optimally in learning.

We know that information is stored in many areas of the brain. Information is stored in various areas of the brain when it is intentionally imprinted in these areas. The more ways you experience Scripture, the more areas you have from which to recall the experience. This has been an intentional aspect of studying Scripture.

Putting It All Together

Integrating multiple intelligences, creative and critical thinking, and the findings of brain research has the potential to increase transformational learning. The brain is divided into areas called lobes. Each lobe is responsible for different brain functions. The occipital lobe (located in the back of the brain) is responsible for vision—thus, incorporating Visual/Spatial activities would activate this area of the brain. The frontal lobe (located in the forehead area) is responsible for our higher order thinking involving both creative and critical thinking and Logical/Mathematical functions. The parietal lobe (located on the top of the head behind the frontal lobe) is responsible for language functions. The temporal lobes (located on both sides of your head behind the ears) are responsible for memory and meaning and hearing—incorporating both Musical/Rhythmic and Verbal/Linguistic intelligences. Other areas of the brain that pertain to the process of learning include the limbic system, which is responsible for emotions, and the cerebellum (or little brain), which is responsible for movement and involves Bodily/Kinesthetic activities.

Thus, the wholistic methods of teaching and learning provided by the concepts of triangular teaching acknowledge the deep interconnections and integration of multiple intelligences and the processes of creative and critical thinking with brain research. Discoveries of how the brain learns help us to understand that the processes involved in critical and creative thinking and in the different ways people learn are related to different areas of the brain. Using the variety of methods for teaching and learning in multiple intelligences and in the processes of critical and creative thinking engages more of the brain and thus expands the potential for learning. Understanding the process of learning guides us as teachers and leaders as we facilitate the faith growth of adults. The chart on the following page will provide a visual representation of this integration concept.

Triangular Teaching

A COMPARATIVE LOOK AT FUNCTIONS OF YOUR BRAIN

INTELLIGENCE	BRAIN RESEARCH	CREATIVE/CRITICAL THINKING
Verbal/Linguistic speaking/listening reading/writing	Each time stories are told or when you write, your brain imprints neural connections, which become stronger in many ways.	Create a feeling of excitement and discovery. Open thinking by telling stories and writing midrash, or other "what if" stories.
Logical/Mathematical patterns/sequence problem-solving dealing with numbers	Your brain seeks to make meaning. When you list, organize, prioritize your thoughts, it helps your brain to make meaning.	Create a list of criteria to make faith decisions. Learn to make connections from your story to the biblical story.
Visual/Spatial visual imprints spatial relationships	Visual stimulation activates the occipital lobe of the brain and calls several areas into use.	Imagine a picture (literal or metaphorical) of the biblical story on paper or in your mind.
Bodily/Kinesthetic moving/using your body	Using your body to process information helps the brain to draw from the motor cortex.	Stand up. Move. Hold objects, and make literal or metaphorical connections to the biblical story.
Musical/Rhythmic dealing with singing tempo/pitch/rhythm	Music taps into the auditory cortex and other language areas of your brain.	Tap out a rhythm, create a song, or sing a hymn that connects the biblical story to your faith.
Intrapersonal going within to make neural connections	Reflection and introspection encourage the brain to pull from and strengthen areas of your brain to make connections.	Take time to reflect on the connections to the biblical story.
Interpersonal synergy lives Together we are better than anyone alone.	Telling your story and listening to other's reflections on it help the brain to pull from two language areas (Broca's and Wernicke's) for a different perspective.	Take time to share your stories with a partner/small group. Listen to each other and make connections to your faith.
Naturalist honoring God's creation learning from the land	Including this intelligence awakens areas of the brain that recognize patterns, sensory perceptions, and object discrimination/ classification.	Make metaphorical connections to natural images.

Gone are the days when sitting around a table with someone talking *at* you is considered learning. We have come so far in our understanding of how learning takes place that we cannot slip back into old habits and patterns. We must train ourselves to understand the process of learning rather than simply the results of learning. Triangular teaching will more fully engage learners with the fascinating and life-changing materials available to us in Scripture. The opportunities to experience Scripture using the techniques of triangular teaching are presented to you in the lessons that follow.

We know that adults learn only what they choose to learn and what they deem useful in their lives. Again, a significant amount of time is spent on connecting the Bible to life and life to the Bible. Often leaders and teachers spend insufficient time on making a strong link between Scripture and real life content. We know it is no longer enough to hear the words or to study the Scripture verse. Unless it connects to our daily lives, it is soon forgotten. True learning is not merely about assimilation of information; rather true learning happens when it creates meaning, value, and transformation on the part of the learner.

Learning is not a spectator sport! Before you continue on with the book, take a few minutes and consider what you have just read. Write a paragraph or two of what the term "triangular teaching" means to you, or create a sketch that illustrates your understanding. Be as explicit as you can—if you have difficulty, go back and find the points that will help you to clarify your understanding of this concept. You will get out of this study what you are willing to invest in it. My prayer is that the methods of triangular teaching will lead you into a more gratifying experience of teaching and learning God's Word.

How to Use This Book

As is my custom, this will be an interactive and user-friendly book. This book is designed to equip you with the understanding of why the methods work. My goal is to have you so competent in using triangular teaching that it will become part of your teaching and learning being. In order to achieve this goal, follow the steps listed below:

1. READ THE INTRODUCTION TO UNDERSTAND THE METHODS OF TRIANGULAR TEACHING.
2. READ THE SCRIPTURE FOR EACH LESSON.
3. READ THE LESSON, PAYING CLOSE ATTENTION TO THE TRIANGULAR TEACHING TIPS MARKED BY THE TRIANGULAR TEACHING ICON NEAR THE ACTIVITIES.
4. GATHER RESOURCES AND MATERIALS NEEDED FOR THE LESSONS.
5. LEAD THE GROUP THROUGH THE PRE-TEACHING ACTIVITY.
6. LEAD THE GROUP THROUGH THE ACTIVITIES OF "ENGAGING THE SCRIPTURE" AND "LIFE APPLICATION."
7. CLOSE THE SESSION WITH PRAYER.
8. ENCOURAGE PARTICIPANTS TO USE THEIR JOURNALS FOR PERSONAL REFLECTION AFTER THE LESSON.
9. DEBRIEF THE LESSONS USING THE REFLECTION QUESTIONS AND THE TEACHING TRIANGLE AT THE END OF EACH LESSON.

The Lessons

The first lesson is a training session that teaches about triangular teaching. The subsequent lessons are Bible lessons that use the concepts of triangular teaching in all the activities.

Triangular Teaching

As you read through the lessons, you will notice that I often suggest an unusual amount of time for an activity. I have been using this technique for years now, which has garnered attention wherever I teach. Saying that you will have five minutes for an activity is same old, same old. But, saying you will have five minutes and 14 seconds for an activity will cause participants to chuckle at first and then get into the fun. The oddities of time make them conscious of getting their task done in a timely way. I do suggest you invest in a timer with a second button, as a timer provides a very objective way of holding participants to task.

You will see a triangular teaching icon beside italicized sections repeated throughout the lessons. These sections contain supportive information explaining the why's of the activities. The activities selected have been selected for a reason. They are in tune with the multidisciplinary approach and will help to add depth, breadth, and faith formation to your lessons.

The elements of each lesson have been designed with intent and purpose. They are:

Scripture
Each lesson, including the Triangular Teaching Training Session, focuses on a specific Scripture.

Materials Needed
A brief list of supplies needed for the lesson is included at the beginning of each lesson.

Pre-teaching Strategy
Pre-teaching Strategies are "learning hooks," or activities that move participants from getting here to being here. These activities are not simply "warm ups," they are designed to lead participants into the lesson. Brain research tells us that covering these various activities removes elements of stress that prevent optimum brain functioning.

Engaging the Scripture

Activities in this section use the multidisciplinary approach of triangular teaching in order to engage the participants with the specific biblical passages for the lesson.

Life Application

I believe Scripture speaks to us every day and has the power to transform our lives. Life Application activities help people connect the Scripture to everyday life. Sometimes these activities will be longer than the Scripture study itself. This does not mean I am skimping on Scripture! What it does mean is that sometimes participants can learn more through application of the teaching than by simply completing an activity to study it.

For Personal Reflection

This section invites personal reflection on a specific theme or insight that emerges from the Bible lesson. Participants are encouraged to keep a journal.

Closing Prayer

Closing with prayer is a way to add God's "Amen" to the lesson. You may choose to pray each week or invite participants to pray as they become relaxed and trust the group enough to pray aloud.

Leader Reflection

The Leader Reflection includes a set of questions to help you evaluate the lesson. The questions will be the same for each lesson. Your responses will not.

Checking the Triangle

Checking the Triangle will help you look specifically at ways the activities engage multiple intelligences, the processes of critical and creative thinking, and ways all these activities are supported by the findings of brain research. Using the triangle will help you

Triangular Teaching

assimilate the methods of triangular teaching, methods that will help you grow as a teacher.

I have included other resources in this book that will aid you in teaching. They are:

The Appendix

The Appendix (pages 177–85) includes forms to identify your learning preference and worksheets for several of the Bible lessons. Many of the worksheets are graphic organizers to help participants organize information in an orderly manner to aid in understanding.

The Glossary

The Glossary (pages 187–89) provides helpful definitions of terms.

The Bibliography

The Bibliography (pages 191–92) will help you to identify resources for additional reading in the theories that are brought together in *Triangular Teaching*.

Additional Resources

Among the items I recommend to use as additional resources are:
• A good Bible dictionary
• A good Bible commentary
• Other resource books with pictures
• Maps of the world in which Jesus lived
• A copy of *The Visual Bible*

I believe we are called by God and given the awesome responsibility of teaching God's people. I wish for you a wonderful journey into making discoveries about teaching and learning God's Word for us in our world today.

Triangular Teaching Training Session

Scripture: Proverbs 2:1-5

Materials Needed:
- Printed words *Brain Research, Multiple Intelligences, Creative and Critical Thinking*
- Tape
- Newsprint/markers
- Pipe cleaners—three per participant
- Copies of the Ways of Learning Profile (Appendix, pages 177–78)
- Journaling materials
- Bibles, Bible commentaries, Bible dictionaries, Bible maps

Pre-teaching Strategy
Have several triangles displayed in the room as two-dimensional pictures and three-dimensional structures. Print the words "Brain Research," "Multiple Intelligences," and "Creative and Critical Thinking" on strips of paper backed with tape. Give three colored pipe cleaners to each participant. Ask participants to tell you the attributes of an equilateral triangle. Record the responses on newsprint or chalkboard.

Hooking the interest of participants as soon as they enter the room provides for a level of anticipation and wanting to know more. This activity incorporates Visual/Spatial, Bodily/Kinesthetic, Verbal/Linguistic, and Logical/Mathematical learning tools.

Triangular Teaching

Engaging the Scripture

Explain that the following Scripture captures the essence of what we will be involved with in this Bible study. Explain that the Book of Proverbs is one of the books of wisdom in the Old Testament. The purpose of the book was educational, and its tone is parental. The book focuses on wisdom teachings that bring together one's experience and interpretation of life with one's actions.[1]

Invite participants to listen carefully and respond with their own understanding of what the Scripture is saying. Read Proverbs 2:1-5. Invite responses. Explain that the next several months will be spent in an in-depth study of the life and teachings of Jesus. Explain that this study of the Christian testament will be interactive and participatory. Everyone will be engaged in, involved in, and responsible for his or her own learning.

⟨ *This activity serves a dual purpose. It connects Scripture to learning, and it provides participants with an idea of what is to come. Alerting participants to the fact that they will be actively involved in their own learning will help to alleviate feelings of surprise during the study. The expectations are stated up front.*

Creating the Triangle

Ask participants what they need to feel safe and comfortable in a Bible study class. Create a list of Rules for a Safe Environment. Invite them to consider what "rules" they would need to have in place in order to feel emotionally and psychologically safe. Record these rules and keep them posted in your classroom throughout this entire study. Invite participants to covenant to uphold these rules and to monitor themselves.

⟨ *When participants create their own rules, there is greater ownership. Participants tend to adhere to their own rules with greater certainty than rules that someone else has established for them.*

Explain that brain research demonstrates a good and valid reason for creating these rules. The brain cannot function optimally if it senses any form of threat. Threat may come in the form of sarcasm, put-downs, fear of little biblical knowledge, fear of looking foolish, etc. In order for the brain to be fully and completely engaged, it must feel safe. Assure participants that they will learn and grow in an environment that is both physically and psychologically safe.

Communicating clearly to the participants about the learning brain techniques you are using will help them to understand why some lessons work better for them than others.

This explanation is a segue into the first side or base of the triangle. Hold up the paper with the words "Brain Research," and tape it to a wall or board as the base of the triangle. Explain that much of what we will be doing is based on how the brain learns. You will be told when and why research into the learning brain is being utilized. Your responses will be welcome. Invite participants to begin to create their own triangle with pipe cleaners. The first pipe cleaner will be the base of the triangle.

Explain that the second side of the triangle is based on multiple intelligence theory. Attach the paper that reads "Multiple Intelligences" as the second side of the triangle. This theory, espoused by Dr. Howard Gardner and his many disciples in the field of education, states simply and yet profoundly that we all learn differently. Each of us has the capacity to learn in many and varied ways, but we have our preferred ways of knowing. In this Bible study, we will respect preferred ways of knowing but also attempt to stretch beyond our preferences and experiment with some new ways of looking at Scripture. Invite participants to attach the second pipe cleaner to create the second side of a triangle.

Stretching beyond the way we have always done things is a neat segue into the third side of the triangle—"Creative and Critical Thinking." Add and attach the third pipe cleaner, saying, "Creative and critical thinking complete the triangle." The participants should have completed the formation of the triangle.

Explain that we will begin today by thinking about thinking. Your brain is created to discover patterns and make meaning—that is its job. In this study we will be looking for meaning in various ways to help in our understanding of the life and teachings of Jesus in the Bible. We will use time-tested tools and techniques to increase depth and breadth of thinking. You will be told why we are using these tools and techniques and asked for your input and response.

Our Ways of Learning

Say something like, "We will be making some discoveries about how you like to learn. Please fill out the Ways of Learning Profile from the Appendix and we will discuss your preferences." Allow participants time to fill out their forms. When choices have been made, ask those who have the same learning preferences to sit together for the next part of the activity. Say each of the following ways of learning aloud, and allow time for each group to gather and sit together:

• Verbal/Linguistic
• Logical/Mathematical
• Visual/Spatial
• Musical/Rhythmic

• Bodily/Kinesthetic
• Interpersonal
• Intrapersonal
• Naturalist

You will undoubtedly find participants who will say, "But I like several of these methods of learning—what shall I do?" Explain that we all have at least three preferred ways of learning. Invite them to sit with the group that constitutes their *most* preferred way of learning.

When the groups have assembled, ask them to respond to the following questions:

• What traits in yourself helped you to select this group?
• What strategies do you use to help you learn something new?
• What are your second and third most preferred ways of knowing?

Allow a brief time of response from each group. Ask participants to look around the room and see how the group is divided. Ask for insights, comments, or questions. Suggest that even when the primary intelligence is used, the second and third choices for learning preferences may be different, creating a unique profile for everyone. Not everyone learns best in the same way. Be sure to include your most preferred ways of knowing since you have asked the class to share theirs. Monitor yourself as we tend to teach in our own most preferred ways of knowing.

Explain that no intelligence is better than any other, although most adults have been programmed by living in this time and place to work in the realm of Verbal/Linguistic and Logical/Mathematical intelligences. A great percentage of adults report that they learn through visual aids. (The world of advertising knows this all too well.) Explain that in an effort to meet those needs, you will be using standard techniques of reading and writing. However, in order to stretch thinking, you will add many visual techniques including, but not limited to, videos, maps, graphs, and a timeline of Jesus' life and teachings. Suggest that

Triangular Teaching

we will use many and varied means of expanding our understanding of how Scripture both speaks to us today and is a useful
and critical guide in making decisions.

*The previous activity engages the multiple intelligences
side of the triangle. It helps participants to learn about
their own learning preferences; and they can actually see
and hear how others in their class learn best.*

Creative and Critical Thinking

Explain that metaphor and analogy are two critical tools for creative and critical thinking. Jesus used these tools as a primary
way of teaching. Suggest experimenting with this next exercise.
There are No Wrong Answers! Each answer can be defended
equally.

Record the words, "Is your faith more like . . ." on a chalkboard
or sheet of newsprint. Under the title, make two columns of the
following words—writing only one pair at a time:

Sunrise	Sunset
Oak	Willow
Door	Window
Meal	Dessert
Rock	Pillow
Sun	Moon
Dictionary	Hymnal

Ask for responses as you record each pair of words. State that all
answers must have an explanation as to why it was chosen. You
may use as many of these pairs as time and interest allows. You
may make up your own pairs as long as the words are opposites
in meaning.

Debrief this exercise by asking how it felt to describe your faith in these metaphorical terms. What skills did you use?

The above exercise engages the critical and creative thinking side of the triangle. It helps participants to experiment with metaphorical thinking in a safe environment, which will open the door to creative thinking and provide a new lens with which to understand Scripture. Assuring participants that there are no wrong answers gives them permission to experiment with creative thoughts. The debriefing exercise is where critical thinking enters the picture. Thinking through why you chose the metaphor and how it specifically speaks to your faith engages your critical thinking skills. This is why "debrief" is such a critical part of the process of learning something new.

Explain that you will be using many and varied tools and techniques that will help to open minds and hearts as you bring the Scriptures to life in exciting ways.

Summarize Triangular Teaching

Review the main points of triangular teaching given in the Introduction. Have participants write a paragraph or two about what the term "triangular teaching" means to them.

Additional Resources for the Lessons

The following resources will be helpful for all the Bible lessons.

Provide **books**, such as Bible commentaries and Bible dictionaries, as references for those who want to do more in-depth study.

If possible, have a **computer with Internet access** available for those who enjoy searching the Web. I find that typing something specific into a search tool such as Google™ or Yahoo!® works well. When I want to search for several versions of the same Scripture text, I turn to www.biblegateway.com. Another useful online Bible site is http://bible.crosswalk.com. As with books, it is wise to check Web resources to make sure that they are reliable and accurate.

Provide **maps** of the region during the time Jesus lived his ministry for those who need to see the area.

Have **hymnals** on hand for those who want to experience Scripture/prayer through music.

These reference materials will give credence to the various learning preferences, particularly those Logical/Mathematical learners who need to have substantial information to make their learning complete.

For Personal Reflection

Provide each participant with a journal—these may be purchased or created by stapling papers together. Print the name of each participant on his or her journal. Explain that these books are private. No one will see them but the writer. They are for the participant to record in any way they choose thoughts and feelings about each session. This will be a weekly practice and be done as part of the reflection each week. Encourage participants to decorate their journals with pictures or Scripture quotations as they see fit. Explain that they may create a collage cover for their journal. By the end of the study, they will have a unique work that is all their own.

Significant insights often appear as people think about what they have experienced in the session. Neural pathways are strengthened as the concepts are revisited and turned into words or drawings. The journals also provide a long-term reference to how Scripture has touched their lives.

Closing Prayer

Close this session with a prayer of thanksgiving for everyone joining this group with hearts and minds open and ready to receive the movement of the Holy Spirit as we learn and grow in faith together.

Leader Reflection

Where did you notice "aha's" during this lesson?

Which activities prompted the most participant involvement?

How/where might you "tweak" this lesson according to the needs of your class?

How did you grow as a teacher/learner through this lesson?

Checking the Triangle

Look at the triangle below. In the space beside the multiple intelligences side, write the ways of learning demonstrated in each of the activities. In the space beside the critical and creative thinking side, write which thinking process is supported by each of the activities. Consider whether an activity will be listed on more than one side of the triangle.

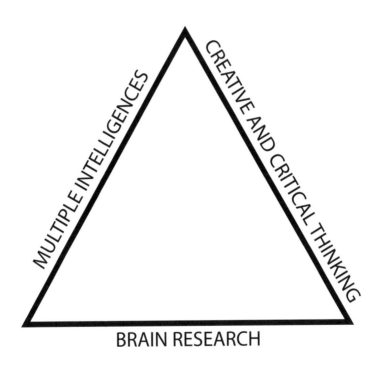

---

[1] See the introduction to Proverbs in *The New Interpreter's Study Bible*, edited by Walter J. Harrelson (Abingdon, 2003); page 893.

TRIANGULAR TEACHING
BIBLE LESSONS

Joseph, Son of David

Scripture: Matthew 1:1-17, 18-25; 2:1-12

Materials Needed:
• Extra Bibles
• TV/VCR
• *The Visual Bible: Matthew* (see Bibliography)
• Newsprint/markers
• Paper/pencils
• Timing device
• Journals

Pre-teaching Strategy

Welcome the participants. Review the Rules for a Safe Environment created during the Triangular Teaching Training Session. Ask participants to tell you everything they know about the Christmas story. Record all responses on newsprint. Keep this newsprint to be completed at the next session.

Break into teams of two or three and ask for the response to: "If you were going to tell someone about Jesus, where would you begin? Why?" Allow for one minute and 16 seconds of discussion. Invite sharing with the total group.

This activity is a learning hook to draw participants into the story. It helps participants to get ready for the opening chapter of Matthew's Gospel. It calls upon critical thinking skills as well as Intrapersonal and Interpersonal intelligences. See my notes about the odd amounts of time in the section called How to Use This Book.

Ask who can recall where the "Christmas story" appears in the Bible. Reiterate that only Matthew and Luke record the birth of

Jesus. Explain that you will be looking at these two stories this week and next week with the expectation of learning at a deeper level what we think we have known all of our lives. We will go beyond our mental scotoma.

Invite participants to read an introduction to Matthew in a study Bible such as *The New Interpreter's Study Bible*, edited by Walter J. Harrelson (Abingdon, 2003). Have extra Bibles on hand for those whose Bibles do not have introductions to each book. Explain that "first impressions" call on our intuitive and/or "gut level" response. Ask participants how they respond to first impressions. Ask for insights and information gained from the introduction. Record the following questions on newsprint or whiteboard:

• Information about the writer—why is this important to know?
• What audience was the writer addressing—why is this important to know?
• What message was intended to be conveyed to the reader/hearer of this Gospel—why is this important information to know?

This information gathering will satisfy the need to know the facts for the Logical/Mathematical learner and will help participants to realize that the Bible has a great deal to tell us in many and varied ways.

Engaging the Scripture

Divide participants into three groups. Invite each group to read one of the Scripture sections: Matthew 1:1-17; 1:18-25; and 2:1-12. Have each group discuss the following: In this Scripture, what challenges you or makes you want to know more?

Matthew 1:1-17

Explain that Matthew introduces us to the stories of the life and teachings of Jesus with a genealogy of Jesus. He takes Jesus' genealogy from Abraham, as his purpose is to prove that Jesus is the Messiah—the anointed of God—who is promised to the Jews. Matthew lists women and some people in Jesus' lineage who may raise an eyebrow. Ask participants to tell you what they know about the following folks in Jesus' genealogy:

• <u>Jacob</u> cheated his brother Esau out of his inheritance and blessing (Genesis 25:31-33; 27:18-29).
• <u>Tamar</u> had an incestuous relationship with her father-in-law (Genesis 38:24-26).
• <u>Rahab</u> was a prostitute (Joshua 2:1).
• <u>Ruth</u> was a foreigner (Ruth 4:10).
• <u>David</u> had Uriah killed because he wanted his wife, Bathsheba (2 Samuel 11:12-17).

Ask, "Why do you think Matthew placed so much emphasis on Jesus' genealogy (such that it was) that he opened the Gospel with this information?" Refer back to the earlier discussion about how you would introduce Jesus—Matthew chose to introduce him through his lineage, providing "proof" that he was the Messiah.

Matthew 1:18-25

Show the clip of the angel visiting Joseph from *The Visual Bible: Matthew*. Ask participants to look for:

• Joseph's reactions
• the angel's visit
• Mary's response

Show only this clip and stop the video.

 This activity meets the needs of the Visual/Spatial learner and of most adults who admit to a greater understanding

*when they have "seen" the story. It also provides an idea of the
dress and setting of the time of Jesus' life on earth.*

Matthew 2:1-12
Visit of the Magi

Ask how many "wise men" there were. Ask participants to search
Scripture (Matthew 2:1-12) for the number of visitors. Ask why
they think we have always seen and heard of three wise men in
cards and songs. If time allows show the video clip of the wise
men visiting the holy family.

 *This activity helps participants to hone their critical think-
ing skills and (if time allows) continues to include the
Visual/Spatial intelligence.*

Invite participants to sing one of the most-used Epiphany hymns,
"We Three Kings." Explain that while this hymn may not be
scripturally accurate (and is the source of much of our belief that
there were three visitors), it is still a viable hymn to tell the story
of the visit of the magi. Explain that many people have come to
think there were three magi because of the three gifts mentioned
in both Scripture and song.

 *Incorporating music engages the Musical/Rhythmic intel-
ligence. It is a powerful learning tool. Singing the hymn
will strengthen neural pathways and reinforce the message
each time it is sung.*

Life Application

Invite the groups to decide if they want to work solo, in pairs, or
in groups of three or four. Ask them to consider and record how
they would introduce Jesus' life and teachings today. What media
would they use? How would they determine their audience?

Triangular Teaching

How will they hook people into wanting to know more? Consider the first impression they will make. They are considering who they are, who their audience might be, and what message about Jesus they would want to convey to their hearers.

This activity provides a Bible-to-life experience that is an important part of transformational teaching and of making the Bible a living document to all those who experience it. The activity also calls upon Logical/Mathematical and Interpersonal intelligences, as well as creative and critical thinking skills.

For Personal Reflection
Invite participants to record in their journals any insights, thoughts, or comments from introductory paragraphs, the birth narrative, and announcement in Matthew 1 and 2.

Closing Prayer
Pray for insight and understanding as you continue this journey of learning more about God's Word for us today.

Leader Reflection

Where did you notice "aha's" during this lesson?

Which activities prompted the most participant involvement?

How/where might you "tweak" this lesson according to the needs of your class?

How did you grow as a teacher/learner through this lesson?

Checking the Triangle

Look at the triangle below. In the space near the multiple intelligences side, write the ways of learning demonstrated in each of the activities. In the space near the critical and creative thinking side, write which thinking process is supported by each of the activities. Consider whether an activity will be listed on more than one side of the triangle. Write any other ideas for activities that occur to you near the appropriate sides of the triangle.

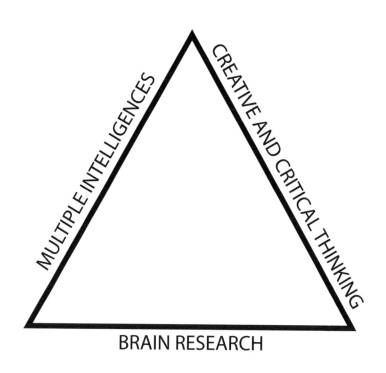

Holy Mary, Mother of God

Scripture: Luke 1:26-38, 39-56; 2:1-20

Materials needed:
- Extra Bibles that contain introductions to the biblical books
- Newsprint/markers
- Hymnals
- Paper/pencils
- Timing device
- Journals

Pre-teaching Strategy

Welcome the participants. Review by asking participants to tell you something they remember from the previous class about the birth narrative in Matthew. Explain that this week we will experience the birth narrative in Luke and compare it with the birth narrative in Matthew.

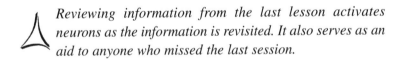

Reviewing information from the last lesson activates neurons as the information is revisited. It also serves as an aid to anyone who missed the last session.

Invite participants to read the introduction to Luke in a study Bible, such as *The New Interpreter's Study Bible*. Have extra Bibles on hand, in case there is anyone whose Bible does not have an introduction to each book. Ask what this information provides about the author of this Gospel that will help us the set the framework for this birth narrative. Ask for insights and information gained from the introduction. Record the following questions on newsprint or whiteboard:

Triangular Teaching

- Information about the writer—why is this important to know?
- What audience was the writer addressing—why is this important to know?
- What message was intended to be conveyed to the reader/hearer of this Gospel—why is this important information to know?

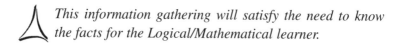 *This information gathering will satisfy the need to know the facts for the Logical/Mathematical learner.*

Engaging the Scripture

Ahead of time, invite volunteers to read aloud. Someone read Luke 1:26-38; someone else read Luke 1:39-56; and someone else read Luke 2:1-20. Invite participants to sit comfortably and close their eyes. Tell them they are about to hear a reading of Luke. Tell them to focus on Mary and listen for new or insightful information. Inform them that there will be 33 seconds of silence prior to and after the readings. Have the volunteers read the Scriptures assigned to them. Remain silent for 33 seconds at the conclusion of the readings. Ask participants what they heard that was interesting, insightful, or new. Then ask for words that would describe Mary. Record these adjectives on a sheet of newsprint.

This experience activates the skills of Verbal/Linguistic and Intrapersonal learning. It also employs the tactic of helping the brain to focus by telling participants before they hear the Scripture what you are asking them to listen for.

Compare Birth Narratives

Create a large VENN diagram on newsprint using the model provided in the Appendix (page 179). Above the left-hand circle write "Matthew" and above the right-hand circle write "Luke." Do not write anything yet where the circles intersect. This will be the area to record information that is common to both Gospels.

Explain that a VENN diagram is a form of graphic organizer that helps one to see items that the stories have separately and in common. Ask a volunteer to read Matthew 1:18-25 aloud to the entire group. Ask the group to listen for insights about this story as they consider it alongside the Luke birth narrative just read. This reading focuses attention and serves as a review from last week and a refresher as participants hear both stories. Divide the class in half. Assign half of the class the reading of the birth narrative from Matthew 1:18-25 and reviewing the words to describe Joseph. Assign the other half of the class the birth narrative as shared in class today and review the words used to describe Mary. Allow three minutes and 14 seconds for this task.

At the end of the allotted time, ask the Matthew group to suggest incidents from the story that appeared only in Matthew. Record these items in the Matthew circle on the left. Ask the Luke group to suggest incidents from the story that appeared only in Luke. Record these events in the Luke circle on the right. Ask both groups to decide on which elements appear in both birth narratives and record those common elements in the center of the VENN diagram where the circles intersect. Debrief this activity by asking for insights.

This activity serves the Logical/Mathematical, Visual/ Spatial, and Interpersonal learner. It presents a visual picture of the two birth narratives and gives participants an opportunity to work together and compare the stories, which engages critical thinking skills.

Sing and Read Hymns

Explain that music is a powerful teaching tool and much of what we know of the Christmas story comes from the traditional hymns we have sung since our childhood. Some of the information is scripturally incorrect, but for the most part we know the story because of the songs. Provide hymnals and invite participants to sing the story of the birth of Christ. Ask them to join their voices in one of the following Christmas hymns that tell the story in words and song: "To a Maid Engaged to Joseph" or "What Child Is This?" or "The First Noel."

Ask participants to keep their hymnals open to the Christmas section and select other Christmas hymns. In small groups ask them to examine the lyrics for scriptural correctness. Ask if the misinformation often found in hymns is a concern and why or why not?

Incorporating music, both sung and read, engages the Musical/Rhythmic intelligence in all adults. Sing as often as time allows in order to integrate this powerful intelligence in the learning process.

Life Application

Think about Luke's birth narrative story in today's world: consider a teenage, unwed mother traveling with her husband-to-be to a place away from home and family. Imagine a cold night and no warm place to stay. Alone, in pairs, or in small groups, write a newspaper article or TV human-interest story about a young "Mary" today. Allow five minutes and 23 seconds to complete this activity. Invite participants to briefly share as they are comfortable.

Relating Mary's story to our life today reinforces the circumstances and complications of the biblical birth narrative. This exercise incorporates the Verbal/Linguistic intelligence and calls upon creative and critical thinking skills.

For Personal Reflection

Refer back to the beginning exercise of "Tell me everything you know about the Christmas story." Ask if there is anything they would like to add or delete from their original list. Encourage participants to record insights and "aha's" in their journals.

Closing Prayer
Close by singing or reading one of the traditional Christmas carols or hymns as a prayer.

Leader Reflection

Where did you notice "aha's" during this lesson?

Which activities prompted the most participant involvement?

How/where might you "tweak" this lesson according to the needs of your class?

How did you grow as a teacher/learner through this lesson?

Checking the Triangle

Look at the triangle below. In the space near the multiple intelligences side, write the ways of learning demonstrated in each of the activities. In the space near the critical and creative thinking side, write which thinking process is supported by each of the activities. Consider whether an activity will be listed on more than one side of the triangle. Write any other ideas for activities that occur to you near the appropriate sides of the triangle.

Remember Your Baptism and Be Thankful

Scripture: Matthew 3:13-17; Mark 1:9-11; Luke 3:21-22; John 1:29-34

Materials Needed:
- Tape/CD of water music and player or fountain filled with water
- Bibles
- Newsprint/markers
- Timing device
- Hymnals
- Basin of water
- Journals

Pre-teaching Strategy

Arrange to have "water music" playing softly in the background or have a water fountain running in an inconspicuous spot, but loud enough to hear.

Ask participants to respond to the first thing that pops into their mind when they hear the word "baptism." Record the responses on newsprint.

Ask participants to turn to a partner and recall and share all they know about their own baptism; or if they have not been baptized, ask them to recall a baptism they have seen. Allow 33 seconds of silence and then two minutes and 11 seconds for this discussion.

This exercise helps participants focus on the intent of Scripture as they explore the concept of baptism—their own or that of others. It engages Musical/Rhythmic intelligence through the sound of the water.

Engaging the Scripture

Form four evenly-divided groups (as possible). Randomly assign one of the Gospel accounts of this event (Matthew 3:13-17; Mark 1:9-11; Luke 3:21-22; John 1:29-34) to each group. Allow time for participants to read their Gospel account silently and then invite one person to read it aloud in each group.

Allow two minutes and 11 seconds for this activity. When the allotted time is up, call the participants' attention the words printed on newsprint or whiteboard:

- Jesus
- John
- Nazareth
- Galilee

- Jordan
- Dove
- My beloved son

Read each of the words aloud. Ask each group to make note of finding those words in their Scripture. Ask someone to volunteer to record information. Read each word, then ask the volunteer to place a *Mt*, *Mk*, *Lk*, or *Jn* next to each as the groups signify that they found the word(s) in their Gospel.

Debrief this activity by asking participants what significance they believe there is that all four Gospel writers chose to include the baptism of Jesus in their accounts of his life. Remind participants that today in the church we place just as high a priority on baptism. It is an important sacrament.

Helping participants to do their own reading and comparison of the Gospel accounts engages critical thinking skills. This kind of activity addresses the Verbal/Linguistic, Logical/Mathematical, Intrapersonal, and Interpersonal intelligences.

55

Life Application
Polarity Management Activity

Explain that baptism is the ritual of initiation into Christ's church. It is a sign of entry into the family of God and recognizes God's saving grace at work in people's lives. Many understand baptism as a sign of God's cleansing and forgiveness. In most Protestant denominations, baptism is one of the two rituals recognized as sacraments. The other sacrament is the Lord's Supper, also called Holy Communion or Eucharist. In many churches or denominations, infants and young children are baptized. They understand baptism in a more communal way and expect the child to be nurtured in the faith by parents and by all the members of the church. The focus is on God's grace through the community of faith. Other churches or denominations practice "believer's" baptism—the baptism of one who professes faith in Christ—and therefore do not practice infant baptism. They express that individuals need to be able to understand for themselves that God saves them through Jesus Christ. Explain that we will be looking at this difference in understanding about infant baptism through the lens of a Polarity Management tool. This simple, but effective tool helps participants to examine an issue from various perspectives. It is an incredibly useful tool to use when a decision must be made and there are opposing views. Polarity Management encourages people to look at an issue from all sides.

Ask participants to complete this Polarity Management exercise. Prepare four sheets of newsprint, write one of the following headings on each:

Infant Baptism +   Believer's Baptism +
Infant Baptism –   Believer's Baptism –

Place these sheets at four different places in the room. Provide a marker at each sheet of newsprint.

Ask groups to remain as they were and work as a team. Assign each group to one of the sheets of newsprint. Provide the following directions:

Each group must record statements that explain ONLY the plus or minus indicated on the newsprint, whether they agree or not. For example, on the Infant Baptism + newsprint, everyone must write a statement supporting the +. Time will be called and the teams will move clockwise to the next newsprint sheet. Each team will have the opportunity to record ideas for each of the four sides of the issues. Explain that the first two time periods will be longer than the third and fourth because many of the ideas will have been recorded already. Ask each team to read what has already been recorded and either add a new thought or place a check mark if they agree with something already recorded.

Allow two minutes and 15 seconds for the first time period. Call time and have teams move clockwise to the next sheet of newsprint.

Allow two minutes and 15 seconds for the second time period. Call time and have teams move clockwise to the next sheet of newsprint.

Allow one minute and 28 seconds each for the third and fourth time periods, calling time and having teams move clockwise after the third move.

After the fourth time period, ask teams to remain where they are and select a reporter for each team. This reporter will read the position taken on the sheet and what has been recorded on the sheet where they are standing. Debrief this exercise by asking for insights about both the process and the content. Ask where participants feel this tool might be helpful in the life of the church, organizations, or families.

The Polarity Management exercise stretches participants' thinking skills and provides a vehicle for them to examine as objectively as possible all aspects of the issue. This is a powerful tool to use any time a major decision is to be made or when there are two opposing sides to an issue. It engages critical thinking skills.

Reflect Upon a Creed and Baptism

As leader, select for your class a favorite creed as they appear in your hymnal. (You may want to read several and select the creed that you believe will reflect the beliefs of your class.) Invite the group to read this creed aloud and in unison. When you have completed the reading, ask for silent contemplation of what these words mean to them.

After the silence, the leader will hold a basin of water and invite people to come forward as they are comfortable, dip their fingers into the water, and touch their heart or head or make a significant sign with the water. As each participant dips his or her fingers, the leader says these words: "Remember your baptism and be thankful." Ask participants to then return to their seats and sit in silence as they reflect on the words of the creed and what it means to reaffirm their baptism into their belief system today as Christians. If anyone has not been baptized, they can reflect upon the baptism of Jesus as recorded in the Scriptures and consider how it might inform their own growth in the Christian faith. Or they might silently pray about what it might mean to them to be baptized.

 This activity serves a multitude of purposes. It helps the Naturalist and Bodily/Kinesthetic learners as they touch

the water; and it fosters Verbal/Linguistic, Logical/ Mathematical, and Intrapersonal intelligences.

For Personal Reflection

Debrief this exercise by restating the importance of baptism both in Scripture and in the faith community. Invite participants to write about this process of remembering their baptism in their journals.

Closing Prayer

Close by re-reading the creed you have chosen, followed by a prayer for living out our promises as described in the creed.

Leader Reflection

Where did you notice "aha's" during this lesson?

Which activities prompted the most participant involvement?

How/where might you "tweak" this lesson according to the needs of your class?

How did you grow as a teacher/learner through this lesson?

Checking the Triangle

Look at the triangle below. In the space near the multiple intelligences side, write the ways of learning demonstrated in each of the activities. In the space near the critical and creative thinking side, write which thinking process is supported by each of the activities. Consider whether an activity will be listed on more than one side of the triangle. Write any other ideas for activities that occur to you near the appropriate sides of the triangle.

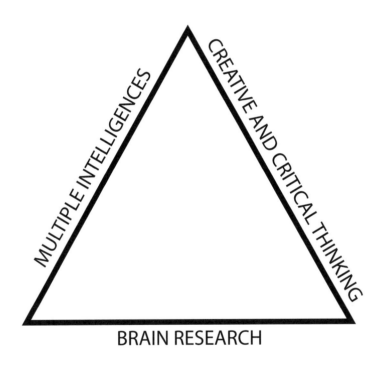

Temptations of Jesus

Scripture: Matthew 4:1-11

Materials Needed:
- Bibles
- Newsprint/markers
- Paper/pens
- TV/VCR
- *The Visual Bible: Matthew*
- Timing device
- Journals

Pre-teaching Strategy

Tell participants you are going to experience a *whip*. Whip is a term for going around the room as quickly as possible with the first word association that comes to mind. Begin at one end of the room and ask participants to respond with the first word that comes to mind when they hear the word *temptation*. When everyone has responded, explain that everyone is tempted by something. Sometimes our temptation is as innocuous as chocolate or as problematic as gambling or worse. Often we overcome the temptations, and sometimes we give in! There is nothing new in the concept of temptations. Going back through Scripture to Genesis, Adam and Eve were tempted to disobey God. Temptations continue through the Bible and include the temptations of Jesus in Matthew.

This activity engages participants' responses to the concept of temptation and sets the atmosphere for the lesson as it opens doors for learning. Assuring participants that everyone is tempted sometimes may relieve stress at a basic level, which is good for brain functioning. It sets the stage for critical thinking about temptation.

Engaging the Scripture

Invite participants to sit quietly with their eyes closed and to listen with their entire beings. Invoke 33 seconds of silence in preparation to hear the Scripture. Read Matthew 4:1-11. Invoke 33 seconds of silence at the completion of the Scripture reading. Ask them the following question: "What, if anything, challenges you in this story of Jesus' temptations?"

Invoking silence before and after Scripture allows participants to quiet their hearts and minds and engage Intrapersonal intelligence through the act of reflection.

Explain that the writers of the Gospels used placement of a particular event in Scripture to emphasize its meaning. Invite participants to read the Scripture before (Matthew 3:13-17) and after (Matthew 4:12-17) the account of the temptation of Jesus. Ask what the group believes the impact and/or implication is in having the "temptations" Scripture set between Jesus' baptism and the beginning of his ministry.

This activity encourages critical thinking skills as participants focus on the sequencing of events. This activity enables the Logical/Mathematical learner to place the events in an orderly pattern.

You may choose to show the video clip of Jesus' temptation in the wilderness in *The Visual Bible: Matthew*.

This activity helps Visual/Spatial learners and most adult learners to "see" the Scripture more clearly and deepens their comprehension.

Divide the class into three evenly-distributed groups. Randomly assign one of the following Scriptures to each group: Matthew 4:1-4;

Triangular Teaching

Matthew 4:5-7; Matthew 4:8-11. Give the following instructions: "Read and discuss your Scripture. Discuss the surface and underlying aspects of the temptations that Jesus faced. Use your creative and critical thinking skills to go beyond the printed words and look for analogies and/or metaphors for what might be represented by the temptations." Allow four minutes and 12 seconds for this activity. When the allotted time is up, ask each group to respond to the total group with their understanding of the temptation for Jesus with which they dealt.

This activity is designed to use creative and critical thinking skills as participants take the written word and discuss it at face value and also go beneath the surface to dig into underlying meanings for Jesus' ministry. This activity engages Verbal/Linguistic, Intrapersonal, and Interpersonal intelligences.

Life Application

Ask participants to think of what these temptations mean today. As they continue to work in their small groups, they will create a scenario that will identify a temptation in today's world with the temptations of Jesus. Tell the groups they will share their creative thinking in any way they choose. They may create an advertisement, a jingle, a script outline, a drama or mime, a song, or whatever method they choose to depict a contemporary version of their temptation. Allow seven minutes and 32 seconds for this task to be completed. When groups have had time to complete their assignments, allow a maximum of three minutes and 11 seconds for sharing from each group. This limitation of sharing time will ensure that each group gets to present their creation. Debrief this activity by asking how it felt to take Scripture and turn it into a Bible-to-life situation.

This activity calls on both creative and critical thinking skills as participants transfer Bible-to-life scenarios. This activity stimulates Verbal/Linguistic learners to use analogy as well as their Interpersonal skills as they work together to create their scenario.

For Personal Reflection

Invite participants to record in their journals words, phrases, drawings, or whatever comes to mind about temptation in their lives and in the life of Jesus.

Closing Prayer

Close with a prayer asking God to help them work through their own temptations.

Leader Reflection

Where did you notice "aha's" during this lesson?

Which activities prompted the most participant involvement?

How/where might you "tweak" this lesson according to the needs of your class?

How did you grow as a teacher/learner through this lesson?

Checking the Triangle

Look at the triangle below. In the space near the multiple intelligences side, write the ways of learning demonstrated in each of the activities. In the space near the critical and creative thinking side, write which thinking process is supported by each of the activities. Consider whether an activity will be listed on more than one side of the triangle. Write any other ideas for activities that occur to you near the appropriate sides of the triangle.

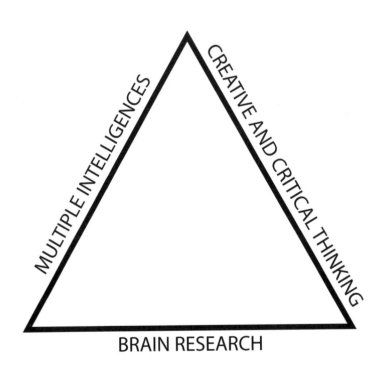

MULTIPLE INTELLIGENCES

CREATIVE AND CRITICAL THINKING

BRAIN RESEARCH

Calling of Peter

Scripture: Luke 5:1-11

Materials Needed:
- Rock, fish, fishnet
- Newsprint/markers/pencils/tape
- Bibles
- Sense circles for the mind map as described in "Engaging the Scripture"
- Timing device
- Journals

Pre-teaching Strategy

Have a fish (or picture of one), a piece of fishing net (if possible), and a rock displayed prominently in the room. Explain that symbols give us visual clues as to people's identity. Ask participants to recall their character development of Peter and how the symbols tell visually about who Peter was. Ask what other symbols might be added to the display to provide a visual portrayal of Peter.

Visual symbols help those who use Visual/Spatial learning to get a deeper understanding of biblical characters and concepts. Asking for additional symbols provides an opportunity for creative thinking and mind stretching.

Explain that knowing about Peter will provide a greater understanding of Peter as one of Jesus' closest friends and first disciples. We will weave the thread of Peter's story in with the story of Jesus' life and teachings. Peter is often at Jesus' side at crucial times and places in the life of Jesus. Ask participants to review what they know about Peter from their character development study.

Engaging the Scripture

Prepare a sheet of newsprint as a mind map. Use the Mind Map in the Appendix as a model (page 180). Write "The Calling of Peter" in the center circle. Write the words SEE, HEAR, TASTE, TOUCH, SMELL in five circles surrounding the center circle. Cut a second set of sense circles out of another piece of newsprint and have them ready to distribute.

Explain that you will begin and end this Scripture reading with silence. Explain that after the beginning silence everyone is asked to read the Scripture silently. Then the Scripture will be read aloud. When the Scripture has been read aloud, everyone will remain silent for a full minute. Begin with 33 seconds of silence. Invite participants to read Luke 5:1-11 silently. Allow a brief time for silent reading. Invite participants to close their Bibles, place their feet flat on the floor, fold their hands comfortably, close their eyes, and take a long, deep breath. Invite them to tune out other sounds and focus only on the sound of your voice as you provide a picture for their mind's eye. Assure them that not everyone will be able to "see" this picture in their mind's eye, and that is OK. Ask them to simply be at peace and listen to the story of the calling of Peter.

Read this Scripture aloud at a slow, but even pace. Add voice inflections as appropriate. (You might want to practice the reading ahead of time.) Allow a full minute of silence when you have finished reading. Invite participants to open their eyes and return to the present time and place.

Silence and listening engage Intrapersonal intelligence.

Debrief this exercise by dividing the class into five groups. Assign each group one of the senses. Invite them to work together as a small group to review the Scripture and record what they might have experienced through their assigned sense if they had been with Peter in the boat. Allow two minutes and 14 seconds for the groups to complete their task. Call time and invite each group to tape their sense and responses to the large mind map. Assure them that there most likely will be overlap and that is OK as we often see, hear, smell something at the same time.

A mind map is a graphic organizer that is a powerful tool for Visual/Spatial learners and is a stretch for those who are learning to incorporate this intelligence. This activity also may expand the understanding of Logical/Mathematical learners as they see another way for information to be organized for understanding. Engaging all senses ensures that this message will be imprinted in several areas of the brain, so that information can be retrieved from more brain locations.

Life Application

Explain that Jesus understood human behavior at its deepest levels. He played on Peter's passion of fishing and promised, "Do not be afraid: from now on you will be catching people" (Luke 5:10b).

Invite participants to look at their own passions (the things that make them excited and the things to which they are deeply committed). Ask them to consider what their senses say to them when they are engaged in their passion. What do they see, hear, taste, touch, and smell? Allow time for this thinking process to take place. They may create their own mind map with their passion in the center and how their senses are involved in the other circles. Allow time to complete their individual mind maps. Ask participants to consider a symbol that would capture their passion and to draw it on their mind map as a visual reminder.

Ask participants to consider and convert their own passion for ministry as Peter did. Allow time for creative and critical thinking as participants make the analogy. Invite participants to share as they are comfortable.

 This activity provides a venue for participants to think creatively and critically about their own passions for ministry based on the model of Jesus' calling of Peter.

For Personal Reflection
Invite participants to consider how their life's passions are analogous to the passion and ministry of Peter and record insights from today's lesson in their journals.

Closing Prayer
Close with a prayer for broadening our own ministry based on passions.

Leader Reflection

Where did you notice "aha's" during this lesson?

Which activities prompted the most participant involvement?

How/where might you "tweak" this lesson according to the needs of your class?

How did you grow as a teacher/learner through this lesson?

Checking the Triangle

Look at the triangle below. In the space near the multiple intelligences side, write the ways of learning demonstrated in each of the activities. In the space near the critical and creative thinking side, write which thinking process is supported by each of the activities. Consider whether an activity will be listed on more than one side of the triangle. Write any other ideas for activities that occur to you near the appropriate sides of the triangle.

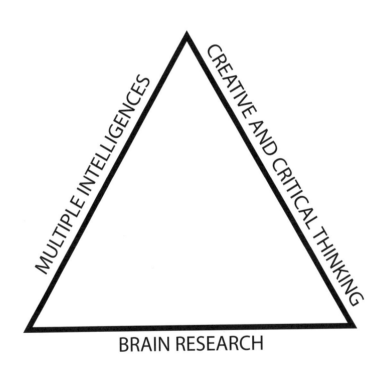

Faithful Friends

Scripture: Luke 5:17-26

Materials Needed:
• Bibles
• Copies of *The Good News Bible*
• Paper/pencils
• Timing device
• Journals

Pre-teaching Strategy

Form teams of two persons. Ask participants if they have heard the term "refrigerator friends"? Explain that these are the friends to whom you could say, "Would you go into the fridge and get the milk?" They are the people who won't care that there is spaghetti sauce on the bottom shelf from last night, or that the jelly jar has as much jelly on the outside as on the inside. These are the people that you trust and love and who you know love you back—warts and all. Invite participants to close their eyes and consider who their refrigerator friends might be. Think about this task during one minute and three seconds of silence. Then ask participants to share thoughts with their partner as they are comfortable. Explain that today's lesson is about refrigerator friends, only minus the refrigerator.

 This exercise uses creative thinking about personal experience to help participants grasp the significance of today's Scripture.

Engaging the Scripture

Please take time to display and share with the class a picture of a home in the time of Jesus. (Search in resource books, children's curriculum, or visit http://www.biblical-art.com.) Point out the thatched roof on most homes. All students, regardless of age, need to understand that the friends in the Scripture were not breaking through a roof as we know it. This important piece of information will help to clarify the story for literal thinkers who may get "stuck" on trying to determine how this could happen, which pulls their thinking away from the story.

Read Luke 5:17-26 silently. As the leader, read this Scripture aloud while participants close their eyes and listen with their entire bodies. Read the Scripture again and ask the class what they saw in their mind's eye. Allow a brief time for sharing. This time ask them what they heard. Allow a brief time for sharing. Then ask them what they physically felt (the crunch of people, pieces of ceiling falling, etc.). Debrief this exercise by asking for insights.

This exercise encourages people to become fully engaged with the Scripture. It favors the Visual/Spatial learner. This activity helps to engage the senses, each of which is housed in a different part of the brain. The more brain components that become engaged, the greater is the ability to retrieve the story and respond to it.

Secure copies of *The Good News Bible* (American Bible Society, 1976) and find Luke 5:17-26. Invite participants to look at the artwork that illustrates the story. (You can also find several illustrations of this event at http://www.biblical-art.com.) Invite them to study the picture and decide who they are in the picture—are they the paralyzed man, one of the faithful friends, part of the crowd?

Invite participants to select one of the following activities:
• Write a midrash (see Glossary) surrounding one of the participants in this Scripture.

75

Triangular Teaching

• Create words to a familiar tune about this Scripture ("Jesus Loves Me" works well).

• Write a headline and article for a newspaper about this event.

• Create a story in prose or poetry about this account.

Allow seven minutes and 47 seconds to complete this task. Allow a brief time of sharing.

 This activity provides choices for ways of learning and for ways of responding. Participants may choose a familiar and, therefore, less stressful activity. They can also choose an option that pushes their boundaries and explores another mode of responding to this story. The story becomes more "real" when people have to respond in their own words to it. The activities engage both critical and creative thinking.

Ask participants, "Who do you think had more faith—the friends or the paralyzed man? Why?" Assure participants that there are no wrong answers.

Critical thinking skills are employed as participants weigh this issue. There are no wrong answers as the answers are their personal response.

Life Application

Invite participants to form groups of three or four (or they may work alone) to consider a real-life situation in which they or people they know have gone out of their way to help a friend in need. After a brief time, invite sharing as time allows.

This activity engages both critical and creative thinking in order to connect the Bible to life. Reflection calls upon Intrapersonal intelligence, and sharing ideas calls upon Interpersonal intelligence.

For Personal Reflection

Invite participants to record insights and learning from today's lesson in their journals.

Closing Prayer

Close with a prayer to help us honor and cherish our refrigerator friends and help us to be that kind of friend for others.

Leader Reflection

Where did you notice "aha's" during this lesson?

Which activities prompted the most participant involvement?

How/where might you "tweak" this lesson according to the needs of your class?

How did you grow as a teacher/learner through this lesson?

Checking the Triangle

Look at the triangle below. In the space near the multiple intelligences side, write the ways of learning demonstrated in each of the activities. In the space near the critical and creative thinking side, write which thinking process is supported by each of the activities. Consider whether an activity will be listed on more than one side of the triangle. Write any other ideas for activities that occur to you near the appropriate sides of the triangle.

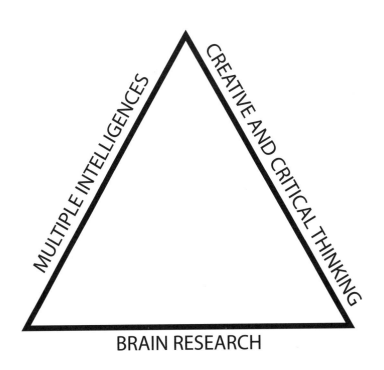

BRAIN RESEARCH

Lilies of the Field

Materials Needed:
• Bibles
• Wildflowers in a vase, if possible
• Paper/pencils
• TV/VCR
• *The Visual Bible: Matthew*
• Copy of *The Message*, the contemporary Bible paraphrase
• Timing device
• Journals

Pre-teaching Strategy
If possible have a bouquet of wildflowers on display as participants arrive. If this is not possible, have pictures of wildflowers in a focal point of the room. Have a sheet of paper at each participant's place. Invite participants to fold their pieces of paper in half; and label one column WANTS and the other column NEEDS. Explain that very often we are driven to "want" things due to the genius of marketers or what our neighbors have. Every once in a while, it is neat to simply make a list of wants and needs. Invite participants to create their lists now. Allow five minutes and 23 seconds for this task of listing at least ten wants and ten needs. When the allotted time is up, invite participants to share their list with a partner as they are comfortable. Allow a brief time for sharing. Debrief this exercise by asking what drives our wants. Allow for discussion.

> *This exercise calls for self reflection in the Intrapersonal intelligence and upon Visual/Spatial intelligence. Creating the list engages Logical/Mathematical intelligence. Use of the wildflowers engages the Naturalist intelligence. Discussion honors Interpersonal intelligence.*

Engaging the Scripture

Invite participants to sit comfortably and relax. Ask them to focus on three important insights Jesus is teaching from this Scripture as they watch the video clip. Show the video clip from *The Visual Bible: Matthew* of this Scripture (Matthew 6:28-34). Invite responses to what they believe Jesus is teaching and record responses on a sheet of newsprint.

Invite someone to read this same scriptural account from *The Message*, by Eugene H. Peterson (NavPress, 2002). Invite participants to listen for three important insights Jesus is teaching as they listen to the words of this Scripture. Ask for responses on the two Scripture presentations—video and spoken word in a contemporary and non-traditional Bible rendition. Record any additional insights from this spoken word onto the newsprint.

This exercise incorporates Visual/Spatial and Verbal/Linguistic intelligences as participants see and hear this Scripture. Creative thinking is incorporated as participants hear this Scripture in modern-day language.

Life Application

Invite participants to return to their lists of WANTS and NEEDS and hold it up against the newsprint account of insights from the two presentations of Scripture. Allow for one minute and 33 seconds of silence for individual contemplation. Ask for sharing of insights as is comfortable. Give everyone a wildflower as a reminder of this scriptural lesson.

This exercise connects Bible to life as we consider Jesus' teachings and our own lifestyle issues. Intrapersonal intelligence is employed. Holding the wildflower engages both the Bodily/Kinesthetic and the Naturalist intelligence.

For Personal Reflection
Invite participants to record insights from this lesson into their journals.

Closing Prayer
Close with prayer for discernment of our wants and our needs.

Leader Reflection

Where did you notice "aha's" during this lesson?

Which activities prompted the most participant involvement?

How/where might you "tweak" this lesson according to the needs of your class?

How did you grow as a teacher/learner through this lesson?

Checking the Triangle

Look at the triangle below. In the space near the multiple intelligences side, write the ways of learning demonstrated in each of the activities. In the space near the critical and creative thinking side, write which thinking process is supported by each of the activities. Consider whether an activity will be listed on more than one side of the triangle. Write any other ideas for activities that occur to you near the appropriate sides of the triangle.

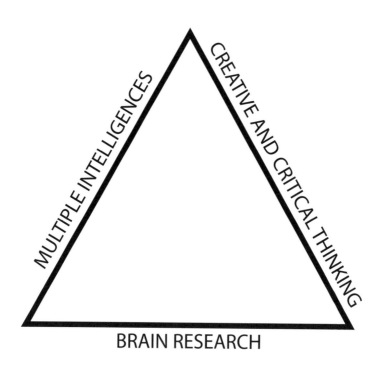

Jesus Calms a Storm

Scripture: Mark 4:35-41

Materials Needed:
- Bibles
- Copies of *The Good News Bible*
- Artwork of Jesus calming the storm
- *The Visual Bible: Matthew*
- TV/VCR
- Copies of the Chart of the Senses (Appendix, page 181)
- Timing device
- Journals

Pre-teaching Strategy
Ask participants if they have ever been in a boat. Ask them to share briefly their boating experiences. Ask if anyone has ever been in a boat (large or small) in a storm. Ask for feelings during a storm anywhere, but particularly in a boat in the middle of a body of water.

Helping participants to consider what it feels like to be in a boat will set the stage for today's Scripture. Such reflection engages Intrapersonal intelligence.

Show a picture of the Sea of Galilee from a resource book, and/or use a map. Explain that the Sea of Galilee is a freshwater lake. Due to its geographical location, a storm could arise suddenly and sweep down the mountains and catch even seasoned fishermen.

This activity uses Verbal/Linguistic intelligence to help participants to get an idea of the location and significance of the Sea of Galilee—also referred to as Lake Genneseret.

Engaging the Scripture

Explain that the Synoptic Gospels (Matthew, Mark, and Luke) all tell this story. Say something like, "We will experience the story through our inner eye as we listen to Mark's Gospel."

Invite a volunteer to read Mark 4:35-41. Invite the remaining participants to listen with their whole bodies and try to get a visual picture in their mind's eye. Ask what other senses kicked in as they listened. Create a chart of the senses on newsprint using the model provided in the Appendix. Photocopy handouts of this chart for each of the participants. After reading and/or viewing the Scripture, invite participants to write about what they experienced in each of the senses. Invite them to share what they have written, and record their responses on the newsprint chart for all to see. Have on hand a few copies of *The Good News Bible*. Have participants look at the drawing of the boat in the storm that illustrates the storm in Mark 4:35-41. You can also find several pictures that illustrate this story online at http://www.biblical-art.com. Ask participants to identify with anyone in the drawing and tell why.

Show the video clip from *The Visual Bible: Matthew* 8:23-27 to give participants an idea of what the lake looks like and how the scene might have unfolded. Ask for responses to the three ways of "seeing" this Scripture (mind's eye, artistic rendition, or video). Ask participants which way spoke to people the most and why. Allow time for responses.

 These activities lean heavily on the Visual/Spatial learning preference. Many adults claim to be visual learners. If they can see something, there is greater understanding.

Life Application

Ask participants to think creatively and metaphorically of the "storms" in their own lives. Ask for examples of life storms—

divorce, job loss, death of a spouse or friend, etc. Invite participants to look again at the drawing in *The Good News Bible* or
other pictures of the storm. Invite them to think about a storm in
their own lives. Ask them to consider where they are in this scenario. Debrief this exercise by inviting insights.

△ *This activity stretches the creative thinking skills as participants use metaphorical examples from their own lives
to connect with the Scripture of Jesus calming a storm. It
calls upon Intrapersonal intelligence in the reflection and
Interpersonal intelligence in the sharing or discussion of insights.*

For Personal Reflection
Invite participants to record in their journals the way they would
answer Jesus' question, "Why are you afraid? Have you still no
faith?" (Mark 4:40).

Closing Prayer
Close with a prayer asking God to help us maintain our faith even
in the storms of our lives.

Leader Reflection

Where did you notice "aha's" during this lesson?

Which activities prompted the most participant involvement?

How/where might you "tweak" this lesson according to the needs of your class?

How did you grow as a teacher/learner through this lesson?

Checking the Triangle

Look at the triangle below. In the space near the multiple intelligences side, write the ways of learning demonstrated in each of the activities. In the space near the critical and creative thinking side, write which thinking process is supported by each of the activities. Consider whether an activity will be listed on more than one side of the triangle. Write any other ideas for activities that occur to you near the appropriate sides of the triangle.

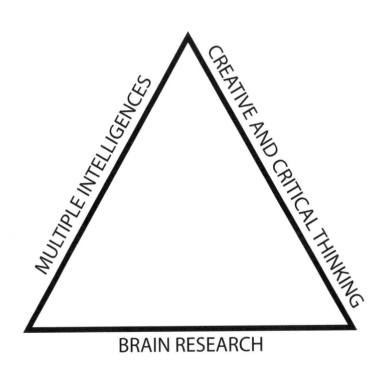

Two Stories of Faith

Scripture: Matthew 9:18-26; Mark 5:21-43; Luke 8:40-56

Materials Needed:
- Bibles
- Newsprint/markers
- Three Bible commentaries, other research resources
- Worksheets of questions described in "Engaging the Scripture"
- TV/VCR
- *The Visual Bible: Matthew*
- Timing device
- Journals

Pre-teaching Strategy
Ask participants if they watch the many medical shows on TV. Explain that the popularity of these TV programs indicates that many people have an interest in health issues. Ask participants what they would do if they had been ill for a long time and doctors did not seem to have an answer. Allow time for and then record responses. Explain that Jesus healed many people in various circumstances. Explain that today you are going to look at two stories woven together and told in all of the Synoptic Gospels.

This activity helps the brain to concentrate on Jesus' healing ministry and on the focus of this Scripture lesson by relating to personal experience. It calls upon both Intrapersonal and Interpersonal intelligences.

Engaging the Scripture
Tell the group that the Synoptic Gospels often contain the same material albeit told in different order and with slight variations that reflect each Gospel writer's perspective and purpose.

Divide the class into three equal groups. Assign each group one of the following Scriptures: Matthew 9:18-26; Mark 5:21-43; Luke 8:40-56. Have each group read their Scripture silently and then have one person read it aloud in each group. Provide each group with a Bible commentary and other resources and have them read what the resources say about their Scripture. Ask them to make note of all items that seem to be interesting and/or important. Discuss their findings as a group and write the findings on a list. Allow five minutes and 23 seconds for this task.

Create a large piece of newsprint with three columns. Head the first column with the word MATTHEW, the second with MARK, and the third with LUKE.

When the allotted time is up, ask each group individually to report what they found interesting and important in their Scripture. Make a list of these responses. When this reporting from the three groups has taken place, invite a participant to come up and place a check mark next to the items that are repeated in more than one Gospel account.

Debrief this exercise by asking participants for insights gleaned from their reading and the composite picture of all three accounts of this story.

This activity provides the Verbal/Linguistic learner, the Visual/Spatial learner, the Logical/Mathematical learner, and the Interpersonal learner with opportunities to use their most preferred ways of knowing in one activity.

If time allows, show the video clip of this Scripture from *The Visual Bible: Matthew* or go to http://www.biblical-art.com and view different artists' renditions of this Scripture.

Triangular Teaching

Create a worksheet of the following questions for each participant. Invite participants to remain in their groups, and ask them to respond to the following questions as they dig:

• Why do you think a leader of the synagogue would beg Jesus to help him?

• What do you know about the woman before and after she touched the hem of Jesus' cloak?

• Why do you think Jesus noticed these two people out of all the people in the crowd pressing in around him?

• Why do you think Jesus asks for the person to reveal herself? "Who touched my clothes?" (Mark 5:30).

• What part do you think faith had to do with both of these healing stories?

Invite participants to work individually within their groups for two minutes and three seconds. When each participant has had time to consider the questions, small groups can share information and then respond as a group. Allow five minutes and 49 seconds for this activity. Debrief this activity by asking for insights.

> *This activity allows further exploration, which leads to creative and critical thinking about the story. Digging deeper helps to reveal more about the story than is simply at the surface level.*

Life Application

Ask participants who they most identify with in these stories and why. Ask them what they would consider doing were they in either of the situations mentioned in Scripture. Allow a full 33 seconds for silent contemplation of this question. Ask each participant to find a partner and share what is comfortable. Allow time for discussion. Ask anyone who is comfortable to share with the total group. Ask this question in a different way by asking participants what part they believe faith plays in healing today. Invite anyone to give witness to their belief as they are comfortable.

 This activity helps participants move from Bible to life through the use of both Interpersonal and Intrapersonal intelligence.

For Personal Reflection

Invite participants to record in their journals something significant about the relationship between faith and healing as explored in Matthew 9:18-26; Mark 5:21-43; Luke 8:40-56.

Closing Prayer

Close with a prayer for continuing faith even in our darkest hours.

Leader Reflection

Where did you notice "aha's" during this lesson?

Which activities prompted the most participant involvement?

How/where might you "tweak" this lesson according to the needs of your class?

How did you grow as a teacher/learner through this lesson?

Checking the Triangle

Look at the triangle below. In the space near the multiple intelligences side, write the ways of learning demonstrated in each of the activities. In the space near the critical and creative thinking side, write which thinking process is supported by each of the activities. Consider whether an activity will be listed on more than one side of the triangle. Write any other ideas for activities that occur to you near the appropriate sides of the triangle.

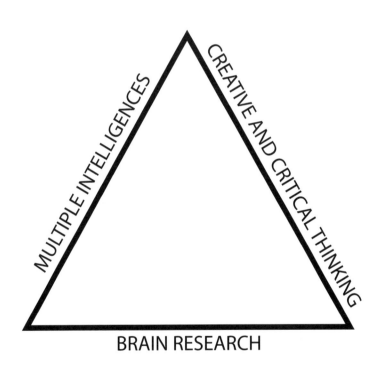

Keeping the Sabbath

Scripture: Mark 2:23-28

Materials Needed:
- Bibles
- Paper/pencils
- Timing device
- Journals

Pre-teaching Strategy

Ask how many participants remember "blue laws." If anyone remembers blue laws, ask him or her to explain this concept to the class. If no one knows what blue laws are, explain that these laws were formed in order to regulate what could be done on Sunday. Businesses were required to be closed and no one was to work. Explain that this reasoning came from the Creation story in the Book of Genesis when God rested on the seventh day (Genesis 2:2-3). This concept of sabbath was revisited in Exodus as one of the commandments given to Moses (Exodus 20:8-11). Ask how the concept of sabbath was regarded as participants were growing up and how it is regarded today. Ask if participants believe this is still a viable commandment. Why or why not? Invite discussion.

This activity calls upon the Intrapersonal and Interpersonal intelligences by having the participants recall what they remember about blue laws. It engages critical and creative thinking as it invites them to compare blue laws to biblical sabbath laws.

Engaging the Scripture

Ask the participants to sit comfortably and listen with their eyes closed. Read Genesis 2:2-3 and Exodus 20:8-11. Then read Mark 2:23-28.

Divide the class into two teams. Have Team One defend the commandment of keeping the sabbath holy (Exodus 20:8-11). Team Two is to defend Jesus' statement that the sabbath was made for humankind, and not humankind for the sabbath (Mark 2:27-28).

Instruct the groups to establish at least four good reasons to defend each statement. Allow five minutes and 42 seconds for the groups to work on their positions.

When the allotted time is up, invite each group to defend their position, giving them two minutes and 11 seconds. When each side has presented their position, ask for a rebuttal from the opposing sides.

Establishing a debate format provides the opportunity for critical thinking as the groups find ways to defend their position. The Logical/Mathematical learners and the Verbal/Linguistic learners will excel in this exercise as it calls on their most preferred intelligences.

Life Application

Explain that, according to *Harper's Bible Dictionary*, the Hebrew root of the word sabbath is *shabbat*, which means "to cease, desist" and is "the weekly day of rest and abstention from work enjoined upon the Israelites." The Bible contains many references to sabbath observances including restrictions from work and giving rest to servants and animals. Such[2] observances underscored the special relationship with God. Consider the idea that Jesus obeyed the spirit of the law as opposed to the letter of the law. Ask for responses to this idea. At the end of the discussion, ask how many participants shop or do any form of work on Sunday. Ask if they have any qualms about keeping sabbath or if they find alternative means of keeping sabbath.

If anyone responds in the positive, invite her or him to share other ways they maintain sabbath. Suggest that perhaps Sunday is no longer the best or only day for sabbath time. Ask for and record any number of ways that participants might observe sabbath today. Ask how their list upholds the letter of the law or the spirit of the law.

Through reflection and discussion this activity calls upon both Intrapersonal and Interpersonal intelligences to explore connections between sabbath laws and contemporary understandings of sabbath. It invites critical and creative thinking.

Reflection

Invite participants to record thoughts and insights about observing the sabbath in their journals.

Closing Prayer

Close with a prayer about finding a sabbath time or place to honor God.

Leader Reflection

Where did you notice "aha's" during this lesson?

Which activities prompted the most participant involvement?

How/where might you "tweak" this lesson according to the needs of your class?

How did you grow as a teacher/learner through this lesson?

Triangular Teaching

Checking the Triangle

Look at the triangle below. In the space near the multiple intelligences side, write the ways of learning demonstrated in each of the activities. In the space near the critical and creative thinking side, write which thinking process is supported by each of the activities. Consider whether an activity will be listed on more than one side of the triangle. Write any other ideas for activities that occur to you near the appropriate sides of the triangle.

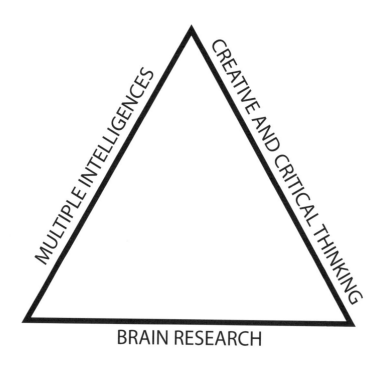

BRAIN RESEARCH

[1] *Harper's Bible Dictionary*, edited by Paul J. Achtemeier (HarperSanFransico, 1985); page 888.
[2] *Harper's Bible Dictionary*; pages 888–89.

Kingdom Parables

Materials Needed:
- Dandelions, or pictures of dandelions
- Bibles
- Paper/pencils
- Timing device
- Journals

Pre-teaching Strategies
Provide a dandelion for each participant (check with a plant nursery in your area). If this is not possible, provide a picture of a dandelion. Ask participants the first word that comes to mind when they see a dandelion. Allow for responses. Then divide the class into groups of three or four (or around their tables, if this is the case) and ask them to come up with as many ways as they can think of that a dandelion is like the Easter story. Allow two minutes and 11 seconds for this task. Invite sharing. Explain that they have just been using the powerful tool of analogy. This is a tool that Jesus used often in his teaching—he took something familiar and compared it to something unfamiliar to help people make the connection.

 This exercise helps participants hone creative thinking skills through the use of analogy. The use of dandelions engages the Naturalist intelligence.

Engaging the Scripture
Explain that in the Lord's Prayer we recite, "Your kingdom come. Your will be done, on earth as it is in heaven." We will make discoveries about what Jesus had in mind when he talked about the

kingdom of God. Jesus used analogy to make this concept understandable to his disciples with varying degrees of success. Explain that the task today is to examine those analogies and translate them into what you believe they mean to us today.

Jesus used analogy in his "kingdom parables." Explain that these are a series of parables from Matthew's Gospel that suggest or begin with the words, "The kingdom of God is like . . ."

Break the class into six groups (adjust numbers depending on class size). Distribute one of the following Scripture excerpts to each group:

• Matthew 13:1-8
• Matthew 13:24-30
• Matthew 13:33
• Matthew 13:44
• Matthew 13:45
• Matthew 13:47-50

Explain that their task is to read the parable and record in their own words an explanation of what they believe the parable says the kingdom of God is like. Ask them to please make this as clear as possible so that others will understand. If some participants would like to complete the task alone, allow them to do so. Allow six minutes and 32 seconds to complete this task. Allow a time for sharing from each group. Debrief this exercise by asking for insights.

Participants use creative thinking to adapt the parable into meaning for the disciples and for today. Working in small groups involves Interpersonal learning. Allowing the option of working alone meets the needs of those who prefer Intrapersonal learning.

Life Application

Have participants remain in their groups and consider what it would mean today to have the kingdom of God be here on earth as it is in heaven. Create your own analogy beginning with the words, "For me/us, the kingdom of God is like . . ." Allow six minutes and 32 seconds for the groups to complete this task. Allow time for each group to share its analogy. If you desire, you may record these kingdom parables and post them in your room or print them in your church newsletter, perhaps including the challenge for others in the congregation to create their own kingdom parable.

 Participants once again will use creative thinking and Interpersonal learning skills to create analogies of the parables in the contemporary world.

For Personal Reflection

Invite participants to record in their journal insights, analogies, and thoughts about God's kingdom.

Closing Prayer

Close with a prayer about living God's kingdom right here and now.

Leader Reflection

Where did you notice "aha's" during this lesson?

Which activities prompted the most participant involvement?

How/where might you "tweak" this lesson according to the needs of your class?

How did you grow as a teacher/learner through this lesson?

Checking the Triangle

Look at the triangle below. In the space near the multiple intelligences side, write the ways of learning demonstrated in each of the activities. In the space near the critical and creative thinking side, write which thinking process is supported by each of the activities. Consider whether an activity will be listed on more than one side of the triangle. Write any other ideas for activities that occur to you near the appropriate sides of the triangle.

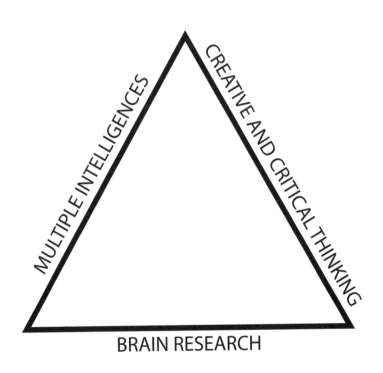

Jesus Walks on Water

Scripture: Matthew 14:22-33

Materials Needed:
- Bibles
- Tape/CD player and ocean music
- TV/VCR
- *The Visual Bible: Matthew*
- Timing device
- Newsprint/markers
- Pens/pencils
- Journals

Pre-teaching Strategy

Have a tape or CD of ocean music playing as participants enter. Have a map of Jesus' time posted in a focal point of the room. Invite participants to form teams of two. Ask participants to silently consider what is the most courageous or foolish thing they have ever done. Invite them to share with their partner if comfortable. Allow a brief time for sharing. Then ask what were some of the feelings they experienced during this act of courage or foolishness. Allow time for responses. Explain that in our Scripture today, we once again find Peter in circumstances that were either very courageous or very foolish.

 This activity draws upon Musical and Interpersonal intelligences to help them identify with Peter's actions. It prepares the brain for deeper learning about the lesson.

Engaging the Scripture

Invite a participant to point out the Sea of Galilee on a displayed map. Explain that often knowing what comes just before and/or after a particular Scripture broadens our understanding, as it provides a time frame and a sense of sequence and order. Jesus had just come from feeding 5,000 people. Jesus had been tired and upset about the death of John the Baptist to begin with; and then he spoke to all of those people and then provided enough food for all of them. No wonder he wanted to be alone for a while. Explain that in today's Scripture you are going to be visiting with Peter again. Invite a volunteer to read Matthew 14:22-33 aloud while everyone listens. Ask participants to sit comfortably and close their eyes for 33 seconds. They are then to focus on the roles of Jesus and Peter as they listen to this Scripture read aloud. Invoke 33 seconds of silence after the reading of Scripture to allow for reflection. Watch the segment of *The Visual Bible: Matthew* that deals with this Scripture.

This activity will provide participants with both an auditory and visual presentation of Scripture. This will meet the needs to the Verbal/Linguistic and the Visual/Spatial learner. Providing the video clip helps everyone understand the Scripture at a greater depth as they view the sea and the intricacies of the Scripture.

Prepare a graphic organizer in the form of a T-Chart. Have a sheet of newsprint with a line across the top and one down the middle (in the shape of a T) prepared and printed with "Jesus" on one side and "Peter" on the other. When the Scripture has been read and the video watched, ask participants to give you words that describe Jesus in these verses. Record responses in the column marked "Jesus." Then ask participants to give you words that describe Peter in this Scripture. Record responses in the column marked "Peter."

Debrief this exercise by asking if they think Peter's actions were courageous or foolish and why. Then ask what insights and/or questions this Scripture raises about Jesus, about Peter, and about the participants themselves. Explain that Peter was the only one of the disciples to have the courage to attempt to reach Jesus. Ask what part faith played in this Scripture.

Using a graphic organizer helps all participants to see the differences and similarities of thoughts posted. This activity helps the brain to create meaning through visual representation and through critical thinking.

Life Application

Invite participants to reflect again on a courageous and/or foolish thing they have done and consider what their motivation was. Often we will do things as an act of courage that we could not accomplish under normal circumstances (a mother lifting a car to save her trapped child, a person running into a burning building to save a loved one, a person standing up for what they believe in the face of danger, etc.). Sometimes we do something foolish to prove a point, like a novice skier who believes that he or she can ski down the most challenging, black diamond hill, even though it is only his or her second time on skis. Consider the part that faith played in your motivation. Ask yourself what you would have done, had you been in Peter's shoes. Invite personal reflection or small group discussion.

Bringing this Scripture from Bible to life will help participants to sort out their own actions. Offering choices of how they want to complete this activity takes away some level of stress, which limits optimum brain functioning. It calls upon either Interpersonal or Intrapersonal intelligences.

For Personal Reflection

Invite participants to record thoughts, feelings, and/or insights about courageous choices in their journals.

Closing Prayer

Close with a prayer for discerning the difference between courage and foolishness as we walk our journey of faith.

Leader Reflection

Where did you notice "aha's" during this lesson?

Which activities prompted the most participant involvement?

How/where might you "tweak" this lesson according to the needs of your class?

How did you grow as a teacher/learner through this lesson?

Checking the Triangle

Look at the triangle below. In the space near the multiple intelligences side, write the ways of learning demonstrated in each of the activities. In the space near the critical and creative thinking side, write which thinking process is supported by each of the activities. Consider whether an activity will be listed on more than one side of the triangle. Write any other ideas for activities that occur to you near the appropriate sides of the triangle.

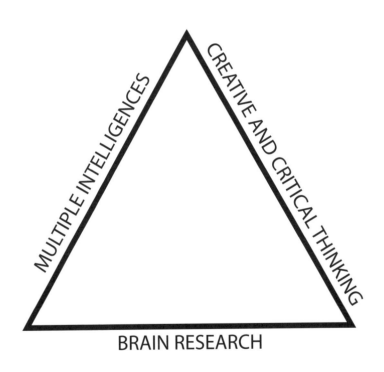

BRAIN RESEARCH

Rich Man, Poor Man

Scripture: Luke 16:19-31

Materials Needed:
• Bibles
• Newsprint/markers
• Paper/pencils
• Timing device
• Journals

Pre-teaching Strategies
Have the participants form teams of two and ask them to ponder this question: "If you were able to communicate with someone who has died, and you were allowed three questions, what would you ask him or her?" Allow one minute and 45 seconds of silence to reflect upon this question. Then ask the partners to share their answers, if they are comfortable. Allow time for sharing and then ask for a general sharing with the total group. Record answers on newsprint.

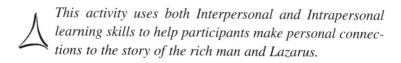

This activity uses both Interpersonal and Intrapersonal learning skills to help participants make personal connections to the story of the rich man and Lazarus.

Engaging the Scripture
Invite participants to read Luke 16:19-31 silently. Then ask them to close their Bibles and their eyes and to sit comfortably with feet on the floor and hands in their lap as they observe 33 seconds of silence and prepare themselves to hear Scripture. Ask them to listen with their whole bodies to the sound of your voice. Ask the participants to form a mental picture as you read. Read this

Scripture with feeling—taking time to read slowly and emphatically (you might want to practice ahead of time). Maintain 33 seconds of silence after you finish reading.

Reading silently and aloud and listening to a reading all activate different areas of the brain. It is beneficial to have a story encoded in as many ways as possible for in-depth learning to take place. This activity relies upon Verbal and Intrapersonal learning.

Divide the class into two groups (four groups if your class is large). Randomly assign the role of Abraham as "Angry Judge" or "Sorrowful Parent." As each group receives their assignment, ask them to consider this story in the light of their Father Abraham role. Allow four minutes and 23 seconds to complete their discussion. Invite groups to share their view of the role of Abraham and reasons to support their view. Debrief this exercise by asking how and/or why seeing Abraham's role through two different lenses changes the emphasis of the story.

This assignment of looking at the role of Abraham invokes both critical and creative thinking. It stretches the mind to work in different ways and analyze the story from differing perspectives. This assignment pushes the Logical/Mathematical thinker to consider alternatives; and it invokes the skills called for in the Interpersonal intelligence.

Explain that this story appears only in the Gospel of Luke. This is a story about reversals.

Ask how the story fulfills Luke's purpose in proclaiming that Jesus came to serve the least, the last, and the lost. Ask the groups to consider the meaning and implications of verse 31. Ask what that particular verse says to them today.

113

Triangular Teaching

Invite participants to consider the following statement in relation to this Scripture: "The window opens, the window closes. Don't miss it."

 These assignments add yet another layer of critical thinking and stretch the mind to consider more alternative ways to view this Scripture.

Invite the groups to remain together and create a modern-day scenario based on this Scripture. They may create this scenario in any way they choose: a drama, a midrash (see Glossary), a newspaper story, a song or rap, or a poem. Allow seven minutes and 32 seconds to complete this task. Invite each group to share their scenario with the total class in any way they have chosen to present it.

 Creative thinking forces participants to make the transition from the Bible to life and to explore ways this Scripture might be lived today. Verbal/Linguistic, Logical/ Mathematical, Intrapersonal, Interpersonal, and possibly Musical/Rhythmic intelligences are called into play as participants explore and turn this Scripture into their own creations.

Life Application
Consider that whatever this story says to the rich man, it also says to us.

Ask participants to consider how this story impacts their lives. Who would be the messenger that would make them change the way they live their lives?

 This activity involves both creative and critical thinking and Intrapersonal learning to help participants connect the story to their lives.

For Personal Reflection

Record in your journal any insights and thoughts gleaned from today's Scripture about reversals or about life after death.

Closing Prayer

Close with a prayer for consideration of our lifestyles and how we might become more loving and giving in light of this powerful Scripture.

Leader Reflection

Where did you notice "aha's" during this lesson?

Which activities prompted the most participant involvement?

How/where might you "tweak" this lesson according to the needs of your class?

How did you grow as a teacher/learner through this lesson?

Checking the Triangle

Look at the triangle below. In the space near the multiple intelligences side, write the ways of learning demonstrated in each of the activities. In the space near the critical and creative thinking side, write which thinking process is supported by each of the activities. Consider whether an activity will be listed on more than one side of the triangle. Write any other ideas for activities that occur to you near the appropriate sides of the triangle.

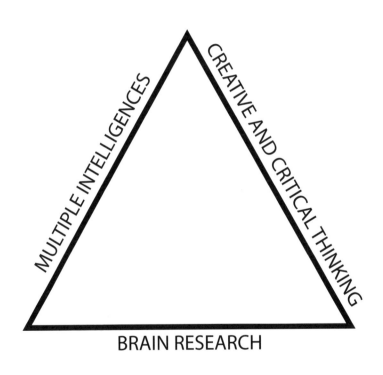

Thank You!

Scripture: Luke 17:11-19

Materials Needed:
- Research resources: maps, Bible dictionaries, Bible commentaries, concordances
- Paper/pencils
- Bibles
- Timing device
- Journals

Pre-teaching Strategy

As participants enter, have the question, "What did you learn about saying thank you when you were growing up?" printed on newsprint and displayed in a focal point in the room. Invite participants to locate a partner and take a minute to discuss what they learned about saying thank you when they were growing up and what it means to say thank you today. Allow three minutes and 15 seconds for discussion. Bring the total group together and ask, "Does an e-mail message count as a thank you?" "Can you simply *say* thank you?" "Are formal or informal notes needed?" Allow for brief responses, and then ask, "How do you like to receive thanks?"

 This activity uses Interpersonal learning to help participants focus on the core theme of gratitude.

Make these clarifications before reading Scripture to make certain to help students understand the terms used in this story:

- *Leprosy*—a variety of skin diseases
- *Samaritans*—inhabitants of the country of Samaria. There appears to have been mutual hatred between Samaritans and Jews.

Divide the class into two groups. Assign one group the word "Leprosy" and the other group "Samaritans." Provide maps, concordances, Bible dictionaries, and Bible commentaries so that participants have access to information. Allow five minutes and 42 seconds for the groups to do their research and compile their information. Give each group time to briefly report back to the total group.

> *This activity uses Logical/Mathematical, Visual/Spatial, Verbal/Linguistic, and Interpersonal intelligences. It ensures that all participants are clear about the meaning of the vital words in this Scripture so that greater understanding of scriptural content can take place.*

Engaging the Scripture

Invite everyone to sit quietly with eyes closed for 33 seconds of silence. Invite a volunteer ahead of time to read Luke 17:11-19. When the Scripture has been read, maintain silence for another 33 seconds. Then ask for reactions. Ask if knowing the information about leprosy and Samaritans helped in their understanding of the significance of the story. Why or why not?

Return to the investigative work done in preparation for reading this Scripture. Using this information, ask participants why they believe one man returned to offer thanks and the others did not. Ask if they can think of any reason the nine men did not return to offer thanks. Refer back to the opening exercise of this lesson and ask what they believe they might have done had they been the person healed of leprosy.

> *Reflective thought using information they have gathered will help participants use critical thinking skills in presenting reasons for the nine men to not return to give thanks to Jesus.*

Life Application

Ask participants to consider at least seven reasons to give thanks for things in their lives. Inform them that keeping a "Thankful Journal" is a good idea to get them centered in a positive outlook on life and in purposefully giving thanks to God. Invite participants who wish to, to turn to a partner and share their reasons to give thanks. Some may choose to reflect silently and not to share.

This exercise encourages the implementation of both Intrapersonal and Interpersonal intelligences. Self-reflection and sharing are two differing activities and often are used in tandem for optimum learning. Assuring participants that they may choose to reflect and not share provides a brain-friendly safety net and avoids unnecessary stress.

Ask participants to close their eyes and focus on someone who has helped them along their journey of faith, healed them in any number of ways, or made a significant difference in their lives. Allow a full minute to focus on this person or persons. Ask participants to speak a one- or two-word feeling about this person. Suggest that they may want to write a note of thanks to this person or find some significant means of offering thanks.

We live in such a busy world that often we don't take the time to say thank you or to reflect on how we have been blessed. An attitude of gratitude helps the brain to produce healing and positive chemicals, called endorphins, throughout the body.

For Personal Reflection

Encourage participants to write some thoughts or feelings about giving thanks in their journals.

Closing Prayer

Close with a prayer of thankfulness for all the ways God has blessed us here and now.

Leader Reflection

Where did you notice "aha's" during this lesson?

Which activities prompted the most participant involvement?

How/where might you "tweak" this lesson according to the needs of your class?

How did you grow as a teacher/learner through this lesson?

Checking the Triangle

Look at the triangle below. In the space near the multiple intelligences side, write the ways of learning demonstrated in each of the activities. In the space near the critical and creative thinking side, write which thinking process is supported by each of the activities. Consider whether an activity will be listed on more than one side of the triangle. Write any other ideas for activities that occur to you near the appropriate sides of the triangle.

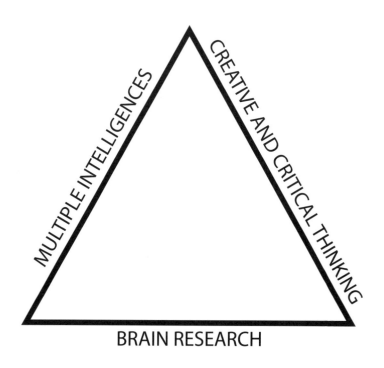

MULTIPLE INTELLIGENCES

CREATIVE AND CRITICAL THINKING

BRAIN RESEARCH

Unclean

Scripture: Mark 7:14-23

Materials Needed:
• Toothpaste
• Plate
• Bibles
• Paper/pencils
• Timing device
• Journals

Pre-teaching Strategies
Bring a tube of toothpaste to class. Ask for a volunteer to come and help you with an experiment. Put a plate on the table and squeeze some toothpaste out of the tube. Ask the volunteer to try to put the toothpaste back into the tube. Ask participants to consider how the toothpaste is like unkind words. After some discussion, suggest that today's Scripture deals with this metaphorical experiment.

 This activity invokes creative and critical thinking as the brain makes metaphorical connections in order to set up the lesson in Mark 7:14-23.

Engaging the Scripture
Invoke 33 seconds of silence before and after reading the Scripture. Invite a volunteer to read Mark 7:14-23 aloud. Then share the following story about living this Scripture.

A personal story: My mother was very wise. She knew Scripture and often used it without quoting chapter and verse. I grew up Russian Orthodox—like our Roman Catholic brothers and sisters, we did not eat meat on Friday. One Friday when I was about ten years old, I had taken my younger brother to the movies. When the movie was over, we were hungry. Near the bus stop was a hot dog stand. I bought us each a hot dog and they were very good. All of a sudden I realized it was Friday. I was sure that I was going straight to hell; not passing Go and collecting $200.00. This realization was not only for eating the hot dog but for buying one for my brother as well. I was so upset that I found a phone booth and called my mother to confess my transgression. She assured me that it was more important what came out of my mouth than what went into it. Needless to say, this wisdom made me feel much better. It was not until many years later that I was teaching a Bible study and came across this Scripture. I was immediately reminded of my mother's wisdom and understanding of Scripture.

Invite participants to form teams of two and consider stories from their own lives that support this scriptural truth of Jesus' words as he explained to his disciples, "Do you not see that whatever goes into a person from outside cannot defile, since it enters, not the heart but the stomach, and goes out into the sewer? It is what comes out of a person that defiles" (Mark 7:18b-19). Allow one minute and 11 seconds of sharing. Invite a brief sharing of insights with the total class.

Invite the teams to create a list of other evils (besides those Jesus listed in verses 21-22) that come out of a person's heart and mouth that cause them to be unclean in the eyes of God. Allow two minutes and 11 seconds for this exercise. When the allotted time is up, invite the teams to share with the total group, record the responses on newsprint. Debrief these exercises by asking for insights for their own lives.

 These activities use Interpersonal and Logical/Mathematical intelligences in order to help participants make connections between the Bible and incidents in their lives.

Life Application

Ask participants to choose to work with a partner to create a bumper sticker, an advertising jingle, poetry, rap, artwork, or any other form of creative expression that reflects Mark 7:14-23. Allow four minutes and 13 seconds to complete their creation. Invite sharing from the various teams of two. The final products can be displayed in the classroom or in the hallway near your room.

This activity encourages creative thinking as participants create in a variety of ways a representation of Scripture. The activities honor the Verbal/Linguistic and possibly the Musical/Rhythmic learners.

For Personal Reflection

Allow time for participants to record in their journals insights or life lessons from this Scripture about what is considered to be unclean.

Closing Prayer

Close with a prayer asking God to help us monitor and be careful of what comes out of our mouths.

Leader Reflection

Where did you notice "aha's" during this lesson?

Which activities prompted the most participant involvement?

How/where might you "tweak" this lesson according to the needs of your class?

How did you grow as a teacher/learner through this lesson?

Checking the Triangle

Look at the triangle below. In the space near the multiple intelligences side, write the ways of learning demonstrated in each of the activities. In the space near the critical and creative thinking side, write which thinking process is supported by each of the activities. Consider whether an activity will be listed on more than one side of the triangle. Write any other ideas for activities that occur to you near the appropriate sides of the triangle.

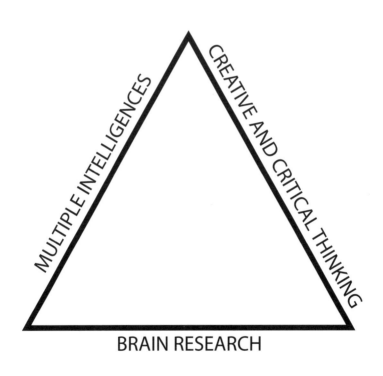

Who Do You Say I Am?

Scripture: Matthew 16:13-20

Materials Needed:
- Bibles
- Copies of "I am" and "I see you as" Open-Ended Sentences and "Who Do You Say I Am?" statements (Appendix, pages 182–83)
- TV/VCR
- *The Visual Bible: Matthew*
- Timing device
- Hymnals or praise songbooks that contain the song, "I Have Decided to Follow Jesus"
- Journals

Pre-teaching Strategy
Provide each participant with copies of the Open-Ended Sentences and "Who Do You Say I Am?" statements from the Appendix. Invite participants to complete the "I am" section only. Allow two minutes and 12 seconds to complete this task. Assure participants that there is no wrong way to complete this exercise.

When all have completed their statements, invite participants to fold their paper in half and find a partner. Ask each participant to hand to their partner the half of the sheet that reads, "I see you as." Ask participants to have the partners fill in this half sheet for each other. Again allow two minutes and 12 seconds for this exercise. At the end of the allotted time, have the partners exchange sheets so that participants again have their own full sheet with both views (self and other) of who they are. Allow one minute and 14 seconds of introspection and thought as participants compare the two views of who they are—self view and other view.

This exercise promotes the creative and critical thinking aspects of participants as they assess who they are and respond as they see others and themselves reflected in the eyes of others. This is often an eye-opening and thought-provoking experience.

Engaging the Scripture

Ask for 33 seconds of silence. Invite participants to read this Scripture silently. Ask for a volunteer to read Matthew 16:13-20 aloud. Ask participants to listen with their whole beings and to form a picture of the scene in their mind's eye. Explain that some adults say they cannot create a mental picture—assure them it is OK—and ask them to simply listen to the sound of the reader's voice. Maintain 33 seconds of silence to concentrate on what they have just heard.

Show the video clip from *The Visual Bible: Matthew* of this Scripture. Ask how their mind's eye picture compared with the video presentation. Ask if it helped them to understand the Scripture message by seeing the video clip. Why or why not?

This exercise engages Visual/Spatial intelligence by giving participants an opportunity to form a visual picture, either their own and/or that of the filmmaker.

In this Scripture Jesus praises Peter and tells him that he will be the rock upon which the church will be built. It appears that Peter has finally "gotten it." Praise the Lord!

Ask participants to consider when or if they have "gotten it"—that is, formed an opinion based on faith of who Jesus is for them. Assure them there will be no need for sharing, as this is a time between themselves and God. Allow for one minute and three seconds of silent reflection.

Triangular Teaching

 Introspection is an important tool of faith growth; and assuring participants there will be no need to share alleviates unnecessary stress. It engages Intrapersonal intelligence.

Explain that there will be one full minute of silence, which will allow everyone to consider the following question: Who do you say Jesus is? Again assure them that there are no wrong answers. Ask them to fill in the last sheet, "Who Do You Say I Am?" (Appendix, page 183). Allow three minutes and 12 seconds to fill in this sheet.

When the time is up, ask for another full minute of silence. Then ask for participants to share their lists as they are comfortable. Record their responses on newsprint. Ask for insights.

 This exercise promotes critical thinking. It requires that time and thought are spent in coming to conclusions of exactly who Jesus is for them at this time and place in their lives.

Life Application

Explain that these exercises might provoke some consideration of behavioral or lifestyle changes. Consider the following suggestions of spiritual disciplines that will deepen your faith and help you become more fully committed to a life of following the teachings of Jesus:

Bible study—To engage in the reading and study of Scripture deepens faith.

Prayer—Make a habit of daily prayer even many times throughout the day.

Fasting—We think of fasting from food and drink; today we might add fasting from shopping, TV, or any other practice that takes overt amounts of time.

Worship attendance—Corporate worship provides a sense of Christian community.

<u>Lord's Supper</u>—Participate regularly in the Lord's Supper in remembrance of Christ.

Sing "I Have Decided to Follow Jesus."

Making a commitment to follow Jesus expresses a desire to make behavioral changes in your life. Allow participants silent time to reflect on what the spiritual disciplines mean to them in terms of their faith journey and commitment to follow Jesus. Singing addresses the Musical/Rhythmic intelligence and expresses an intention in a meaningful way.

For Personal Reflection

Allow time for participants to record in their journals any insights, thoughts, feelings, or actions that have come out of exploring who Jesus is in our lives.

Closing Prayer

Close with praying the song "I Have Decided to Follow Jesus." To pray a song, simply read the words as a prayer in unison.

Leader Reflection

Where did you notice "aha's" during this lesson?

Which activities prompted the most participant involvement?

How/where might you "tweak" this lesson according to the needs of your class?

How did you grow as a teacher/learner through this lesson?

Checking the Triangle

Look at the triangle below. In the space near the multiple intelligences side, write the ways of learning demonstrated in each of the activities. In the space near the critical and creative thinking side, write which thinking process is supported by each of the activities. Consider whether an activity will be listed on more than one side of the triangle. Write any other ideas for activities that occur to you near the appropriate sides of the triangle.

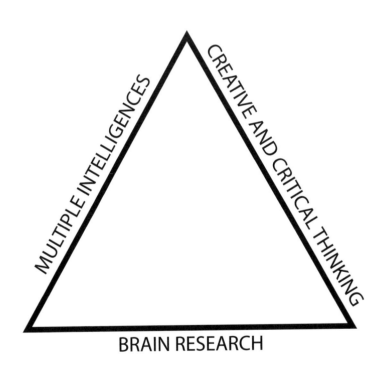

Zacchaeus

Scripture: Luke 19:1-10

Materials Needed:
- Bibles
- Paper/pens
- Picture of a human brain
- Words and movements to "Zacchaeus Was a Wee Little Man"
- Timing device
- Journal

Pre-teaching Strategies
Display a picture of a human brain. Explain that we are going to look at Scripture with both hemispheres of our brain today. Explain that each brain is divided in half, and the halves are connected by the corpus callosum. Traditionally, most people have considered the left hemisphere to control the rational, semantic, and cognitive aspects of thinking; while the right hemisphere controls the creative, musical, and poetic aspects of thinking. Today we know that for true and comprehensive learning to take place, we need to engage both hemispheres of the brain. That is our task today as we look at Scripture from both hemispheres of our brain.

 This activity will help participants to experience and integrate the concepts of left- and right-brained activities. It will also lead us into today's Scripture.

Engaging the Scripture
Ask participants to sit comfortably and invoke 33 seconds of silence as they prepare to hear Scripture. Invite someone to read aloud the story of Zacchaeus in Luke 19:1-10. Ask participants to

listen with their entire bodies to the story. Invoke 33 seconds of silence after the reading of Scripture

Explain that you will begin by sharing left-brained information with your class. Provide the following information and facts.

• This story is found only in Luke's Gospel and is in keeping with Luke's focus on the least, the last, and the lost.

• This is the only reference to "chief tax collector." Since only the tax collector knew what amount was required by Rome, Zacchaeus could collect any amount of money he wanted and pocket the rest.

• Jericho was situated on a major trade route, which meant there were many people to tax. Zacchaeus became very wealthy and very much despised by his fellow Jews.

• Jesus summoned Zacchaeus by name and ate at his home

• For Jesus to go to Zacchaeus' home was improper in the eyes of the Jews, as Zacchaeus was considered a sinner—and one did not eat with sinners.

• The promise to return four times what was stolen is perhaps a reference to the Old Testament requirement of restoring four sheep for each one that was stolen (Exodus 22:1).

• The position of this story (immediately following Jesus' restoring sight to the blind man outside of Jericho) sets up the story of Zacchaeus. Together the stories provide a double proclamation that Jesus is the Messiah, the bringer of salvation.

Triangular Teaching

• Zacchaeus' promises to contribute to the poor and restore four-fold those wrongfully treated stand in sharp contrast to the response of the rich young ruler which appears just a few verses earlier in Luke 18:18-30. If time allows read the story of the rich young ruler and ask for contrasts. Ask participants to consider this information.

Continue with the following information, "We are now going to experience this same Scripture through the right hemisphere of our brain. You may answer as you feel comfortable, or simply consider your answers in your heart."

• Scripture tells us that Zacchaeus wanted to see Jesus. Consider when or how have you wanted to see Jesus.

• Scripture describes Zacchaeus as short in stature. Consider a time when have you felt "short" or that you do not fit in.

• Scripture tells us that Zacchaeus used some creative thinking as he ran ahead and climbed a tree. What creative steps have you taken to really "see" Jesus?

• Scripture tells us that Jesus stopped under Zacchaeus' tree. Consider where or how Jesus found you.

• Scripture tells us that Jesus knew Zacchaeus' name. What feelings are evoked knowing that Jesus knows your name?

• Scripture tells us that Zacchaeus became a transformed man as he climbed down from that tree. What you might describe as a transforming moment in your life?

• Scripture tells us Zacchaeus gave back four times what he had stolen. Consider a "wrong" that you need to make right.

Debrief this exercise by asking for insights about experiencing the same Scripture through each hemisphere of the brain.

> *This exercise is a consciousness-raising activity to help participants become aware of the power and potential of incorporating a whole-brained approach to teaching.*

Tell the group to stretch their thinking and allow themselves to become childlike in order to learn about Scripture through mind and body. Ask how many participants learned the song about Zacchaeus when they were in church school. If they recall it, invite them to lead the group; if not, explain that they will experience something new. Find words and movements to the children's song "Zacchaeus Was a Wee Little Man." Sing and act out the movements to this song.

> *This activity calls upon the Bodily/Kinesthetic and Musical/Rhythmic intelligences. Musical/Rhythmic is arguably the most powerful intelligence.*

Invite participants to work alone or in small groups and write a midrash (see Glossary) of Zacchaeus' transformation. Allow six minutes and 18 seconds for this task. When the allotted time is up, invite sharing as is comfortable.

> *Creative thinking and Verbal/Linguistic intelligence are called upon to write a midrash about Zacchaeus. Offering choices as to how to accomplish this task will ease stress and create a more brain-friendly task.*

Life Application
Invite participants to consider their right-brained—reflective—answers to the questions. Ask them to think about their answers

and focus on a wrong that they need to make right in their own lives. Ask them to consider an action plan for righting this wrong. Assure participants that there is no need to share this experience. It is between them and God.

 This activity brings the Bible to life through the appeal to Intrapersonal intelligence.

For Personal Reflection

Invite participants to think about studying the story of Zacchaeus using concepts of left-, right-, and whole-brained learning. Ask how it felt and what ways it might have expanded their learning. These thoughts and insights can be recorded in their journal.

Closing Prayer

Pray for God's continuing support during time of transformation in our lives.

Leader Reflection

Where did you notice "aha's" during this lesson?

Which activities prompted the most participant involvement?

How/where might you "tweak" this lesson according to the needs of your class?

How did you grow as a teacher/learner through this lesson?

Checking the Triangle

Look at the triangle below. In the space near the multiple intelligences side, write the ways of learning demonstrated in each of the activities. In the space near the critical and creative thinking side, write which thinking process is supported by each of the activities. Consider whether an activity will be listed on more than one side of the triangle. Write any other ideas for activities that occur to you near the appropriate sides of the triangle.

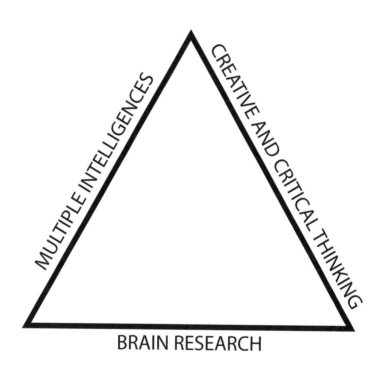

Can He Do That?

Scripture: Matthew 20:1-16

Materials Needed:
- Bibles
- TV/VCR
- *The Visual Bible: Matthew*
- Paper/pencils
- Newsprint/markers
- Timing device
- Journals

Pre-teaching Strategy
Ask participants what they think is the most unfair practice in business today and why. Allow a brief discussion. Explain that today's Scripture is arguably one of the most irritating and seemingly unfair in the New Testament.

A true story: An author was leading a training seminar for a good-sized church that was considering adopting a new mission/ministry program for the coming year. The ministry would deal with a specific plan and training program for reaching out into the community and helping those in need. A seminar was arranged to acquaint the leaders of the church with this new project. The author came in from out of town and did not know any of the participants. This is proof once again that God does have a sense of humor. Leaders of the church gathered and seated themselves at tables around the room. Several Scripture passages were handed out randomly at these tables. Seated at the same table were the president of a bank, the president of the local downtown merchants association, and the owner of the only manufacturing plant in town. They received the Scripture we will study today. To say

141

they were upset would be an understatement. This Scripture flies in the face of all we know about fair business practices, fair labor practices, and employment today. Listen and consider what you would have done if you were the leader.

> Since this Scripture flies in the face of our reality, it is interesting to see how people react to it as God's reality for God's kingdom. This story calls upon both Intrapersonal and Interpersonal intelligence through reflection and discussion as it sets the scene for today's lesson.

Engaging the Scripture

Invoke 33 seconds of silence. Invite participants to read Matthew 20:1-16 silently. Ask participants what their first reaction is to this story and why.

Watch the video segment on this Scripture in *The Visual Bible: Matthew* and ask how physically seeing this Scripture affects them.

Explain that you will be using a technique called improvisational drama, or "improv" (see definition in Glossary). Ask for volunteers to play the roles. Allow them a few minutes to review the Scripture, pull key phrases, and get into their characters. If your class is small or you do not have participants willing to take on these roles you may resort to a reader's theater with participants reading the parts from Scripture.

While volunteers are preparing themselves to play their parts, ask the remainder of the class to return to the story about the author who randomly gave this Scripture to the table with the business leaders of the community for a mission/ministry project. Decide what you would have said to them and what you might say to a group of business leaders in your town today about this Scripture. Allow two minutes and five seconds for this discussion.

Taking the Bible to life and life to the Bible is often an illuminating exercise and helps us to realize that the concepts remain the same for thousands of years. The Bible provides a glimpse of the justice and fairness of God. This discussion activity calls for Interpersonal intelligence and engages both critical and creative thinking skills to make connections between life and the Scripture.

Present the improv drama with volunteers portraying the owner of a factory, the first chosen workers, second chosen workers, the last chosen workers, and a union representative, all as they might appear in our world of business today. Invite the players to portray their characters in their own words. Invite the remaining participants to be the audience, and let the drama begin.

Debrief the drama by asking the players how they felt as their character. Ask the audience how they reacted to this drama. Invite opinions to support God as the owner of the vineyard. Ask participants how it felt to support this idea of God's kingdom.

Because improvisational drama has no script, it necessitates the critical and creative thinking of the players. Drama frequently engages Bodily/Kinesthetic intelligence through movement and gesture. Often personalities are revealed when participants become the persons they are portraying.

Life Application
Invite participants to review their discussion about the mission/ministry project and add to it the reaction to the drama and consider five right answers to the question, "How can we live as God's will be done on earth as it is in heaven?" Ask for one minute and 11 seconds of silence for contemplation and then sharing as is comfortable. Record responses and encourage participants to find ways they can live out God's will in their lives today.

For Personal Reflection

Invite participants to record reactions about the story in Matthew 20:1-16 in their journals.

Closing Prayer

Close with a prayer about considering God's kingdom and how it might affect us here on earth.

Leader Reflection

Where did you notice "aha's" during this lesson?

Which activities prompted the most participant involvement?

How/where might you "tweak" this lesson according to the needs of your class?

How did you grow as a teacher/learner through this lesson?

Checking the Triangle

Look at the triangle below. In the space near the multiple intelligences side, write the ways of learning demonstrated in each of the activities. In the space near the critical and creative thinking side, write which thinking process is supported by each of the activities. Consider whether an activity will be listed on more than one side of the triangle. Write any other ideas for activities that occur to you near the appropriate sides of the triangle.

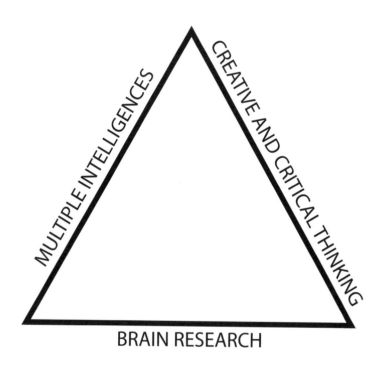

A Widow's Offering

Scripture: Mark 12:41-44

Materials Needed:
• Bibles
• Paper/pencils
• Newsprint/markers
• Timing device
• Copies of quotations cut into single quotation strips, see "Life Application"
• Journals

Pre-teaching Strategy
Form teams of five or six participants as they enter—color coding works well. If your group is small, you may form teams of two. Inform the teams that for all of their hard work as Christian believers, their team has been awarded $100,000.00. Explain that they will have seven minutes and 16 seconds to decide how to spend this amount of money. The caveat is that each team must form a consensus. Following the allotted time, invite each group to report on how they elected to spend their money and record responses on newsprint. Put check marks beside each item that is mentioned more than once and/or from more than one group.

When the reporting is completed, debrief by asking for insights gleaned from this exercise. Note how many groups tithed or gave some portion of their money to the church.

Explain that financial experts often say they can tell a lot about a person by looking at their checkbook. Invite discussion about this assertion.

Triangular Teaching

This activity promotes critical thinking and the Interpersonal intelligence as the group needs to work together to come to a consensus. Consideration of this Scripture tells much about who and whose we are. As each group struggles with how to allot this money, their values come into play. Critical thinking skills are employed as participants struggle together with values as Christians.

Engaging the Scripture

Invite participants to listen for insights about giving that are embedded in these few verses that they are about to hear. Invite someone to read Mark 12:41-44 aloud once participants have been seated comfortably and have closed their eyes. Allow 33 seconds of silence prior to and following the reading of Scripture. Invite responses as to the insights that participants heard.

By directing participants to listen for specific information, the brain becomes focused and is more apt to seek out information than had they simply been asked to listen.

Provide the following choices and invite participants to select one. Explain that they may work alone or in teams of two or more to complete one of the following activities:

• Write a midrash (see Glossary) about this woman.
• Write a story/newspaper article about a woman in similar circumstances in today's culture.
• Create a song or rap about this story.
• Draw a picture about this woman—concrete or abstract.
• Create a slogan and outline of your stewardship campaign around this Scripture.

Allow seven minutes and 59 seconds to complete these activities. When the allotted time is up, ask for groups to share their creative responses with the whole class. Debrief this exercise by asking for insights.

Providing choices allows participants to respond out of their most comfortable and preferred ways of knowing, or they may choose to stretch their thinking and create something that will push their creativity and expand their view of the meaning of the Scripture.

Life Application

Explain that you will be providing quotations concerning money. Explain that the task is to consider the quotation and decide what it says to our world today. Write the following quotations on strips of paper, one per strip of paper. Have your group form teams of two or more. They may also choose to work alone. Give each team or individual one of the following quotations:

• "It is better to live rich than to die rich." —*Samuel Johnson* [1]

• "Put your money where your mouth is." —*Anonymous*

• "Never work just for money or for power. They won't save your soul or help you sleep at night." —*Marian Wright Edelman* [2]

• "The holy passion of Friendship is of so sweet and steady and loyal and enduring a nature that it will last through a whole lifetime, if not asked to lend money." —*Mark Twain* [3]

• "Money often costs too much." —*Ralph Waldo Emerson* [4]

Allow three minutes and 45 seconds to discuss the quotation they have chosen or been assigned. Invite participants to share their quotation and a brief response to what they think it says to us today.

Triangular Teaching

Reading and interpreting invites creative and critical thinking as participants work to translate the quotations into their own understanding. Being allowed to choose the way they will work provides a sense of ease and removes the stress that may stifle creative thought. Verbal/Linguistic intelligence is employed as the activity presents the opportunity to play with words and use their interpretations.

For Personal Reflection

Have participants record in their journals any insights, feelings, or thoughts they have about the use of money.

Closing Prayer

Close with a prayer asking God to help us give from our hearts to help others.

Leader Reflection

Where did you notice "aha's" during this lesson?

Which activities prompted the most participant involvement?

How/where might you "tweak" this lesson according to the needs of your class?

How did you grow as a teacher/learner through this lesson?

Checking the Triangle

Look at the triangle below. In the space near the multiple intelligences side, write the ways of learning demonstrated in each of the activities. In the space near the critical and creative thinking side, write which thinking process is supported by each of the activities. Consider whether an activity will be listed on more than one side of the triangle. Write any other ideas for activities that occur to you near the appropriate sides of the triangle.

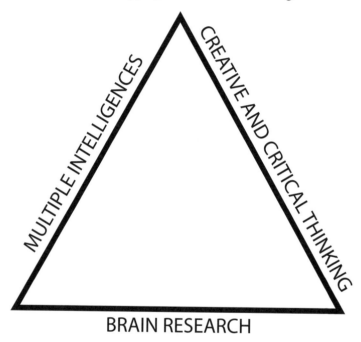

BRAIN RESEARCH

[1] Quotation available from: http://www.quotationspage.com/quotes/Samuel_Johnson/ (QuotationsPage.com, 1994–2005).

[2] Quotation available from: http://www.brainyquote.com/quotes/quotes/m/marian-wrig131694.html (BrainyMedia.com, 2006).

[3] From *Pudd'nhead Wilson*, by Mark Twain; available from: http://www.quotationspage.com/quotes/Mark_Twain/91 (QuotationsPage.com, 1994–2005).

[4] Quotation available from: http://www.brainyquote.com/quotes/quotes/r/ralphwaldo135027.html (BrainyMedia.com, 2006).

Peter's Denial

Scripture: Matthew 26:31-35, 69-75

Materials Needed:
• Newsprint/markers
• Envelopes containing statements on strips of paper as described in "Engaging the Scripture"
• Timing device
• Bibles
• Journals

Pre-teaching Strategies
Print the words "Denial is not a river in Egypt" on newsprint that is the focal point when participants enter the room. Invite them to respond with the first word that enters their mind as they think of the word "denial." Record their responses.

Explain that denial is not a new concept. As we have experienced it in our own lives, so did Peter in today's Scripture. Once again, we find Peter in the middle of the Scripture. And once again, he has gotten himself into trouble.

This activity uses creative thinking in the brainstorming activity and also uses a pun in order to level the playing field and place everyone in the category of "been there, done that." This information helps Scripture to become more personal and the brain more accepting of the knowledge that is coming.

Engaging the Scripture
Assign reading parts for a narrator, Jesus, Peter, and the accusers in Matthew 26:31-35, 69-75. Also assign the lines referring to the rooster's crow in verses 74 and 75. This person will take his or her

cue from the narrator. Allow a few minutes for the readers to look over their parts. Ask them to take on their roles and put emotion and drama into their reading. They will be presenting their reader's theater of the drama a bit later in the lesson.

Divide your class into two or three teams. Copy the statements below onto small strips of paper. Put these strips into an envelope. Give an envelope containing the statements to each of the teams.

They sing a hymn and go out to the Mount of Olives.
The disciples all wonder who it will be.
Jesus is silent.
Jesus breaks the bread and shares it with them.
Judas asks if it is him.
Peter says he will never fall away.
Jesus prays for God's will to be done.
The rooster crows.
Judas betrays Jesus with a kiss.
Jesus tells them they will all scatter like sheep without a shepherd.
Jesus tells his disciples to secure a room for their Passover meal.
Jesus is taken to Caiaphas.
Jesus gives them the wine of the new covenant.
Jesus tells them that one of them will betray him.

Explain that the event leading up to this point is that Jesus has been anointed with expensive perfumed oil. Now you will enter the story and discover the sequence of events to follow. All of the above events take place in Matthew 26:17-75.

Explain to the groups that they each have a series of statements about what happened. Ask participants to place the events in the order they believed the events occurred. Tell them no Bibles are to be used for this task. Tell the groups they will have two minutes and 23 seconds to complete this task. Set your timer and say Go.

At the end of the allotted time, invite someone to open their Bible and read aloud and slowly Matthew 26:17-75. While the Scripture is being read, have the groups make any adjustments to the order of the statements they have just completed. Ask the volunteer to read the Scripture again as participants check for accuracy in their sequencing of the Scripture.

This activity calls on the skills of Logical/Mathematical learners and the need of the brain to create order. Being fully involved, participants must use critical thinking skills as they place events in their proper sequence. This activity also sets the scene for the primary Scripture, helping the brain to create the order and sequence.

Invite participants to sit quietly and focus on the voices as they listen to the dramatic reading of Matthew 26:31-35, 69-75. Debrief this activity by asking for insights and new understanding.

Drama or dramatic reading will call those who are more extroverted to play the roles, but all participants will gain a different perspective from seeing the story portrayed up close and personal. The skill and ability of the players will add depth to the story in a way that reading aloud or silently will not provide. Drama will often engage the Bodily/Kinesthetic intelligence through the use of gesture and movement. It calls upon creative thinking as readers interpret the emotions and events in the biblical text.

Life Application

Explain that just like Peter, we often deny Jesus by words or actions. Invite participants to think about when or how they have denied Jesus. Make certain to inform participants that this may be a very private time or they may wish to share in the group. Assure them that they will make that choice. Tell them there will be one minute and 11 seconds of silence and then anyone who wishes to may speak.

The assurance that no sharing is required will put stress to rest and allow participants to open both heart and mind to this query. This reflection time calls upon Intrapersonal intelligence.

For Personal Reflection

Invite participants write or draw in their journals about their responses to the theme of denial in Matthew 26:31-35, 69-75.

Closing Prayer

Close with a prayer asking for guidance in expressing our loyalty to Jesus in our thoughts, words, and actions.

Leader Reflection

Where did you notice "aha's" during this lesson?

Which activities prompted the most participant involvement?

How/where might you "tweak" this lesson according to the needs of your class?

How did you grow as a teacher/learner through this lesson?

Checking the Triangle

Look at the triangle below. In the space near the multiple intelligences side, write the ways of learning demonstrated in each of the activities. In the space near the critical and creative thinking side, write which thinking process is supported by each of the activities. Consider whether an activity will be listed on more than one side of the triangle. Write any other ideas for activities that occur to you near the appropriate sides of the triangle.

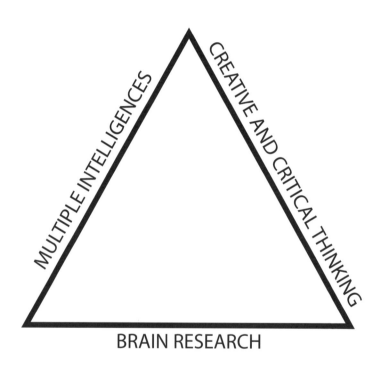

The Empty Tomb

Scripture: Matthew 28:1-8; Mark 16:1-8; Luke 24:1-12; John 20:1-10

Materials Needed:
- Flat stone about the size of a quarter for each participant
- Bibles
- Copies of Empty Tomb worksheet (Appendix, page 184)
- Pencils/markers
- Newsprint
- Timing device
- Hymnals
- Journals

Pre-teaching Strategy

Have a rough stone for each participant to take as they enter. Ask participants to take a stone and hold it as they think about the most incredible story they have ever heard. Invite them to find a partner and talk about their most incredible story. Allow two minutes and 43 seconds for sharing. Call the group back together and ask why the stories were incredible. Record a list of commonalities for "incredibleness" on newsprint. Explain that today's Scripture is one that most people would find totally incredible—yet we faithfully know it happened.

Many Christians find the resurrection of Jesus to be a heart and faith issue as opposed to a head and thinking issue. Few are willing to take on the challenge of providing a rational and worldly explanation. Opening the session in this manner helps participants to know the challenge of faith in the Resurrection. The activity uses intelligences of the Bodily/Kinesthetic and the Naturalist with the stone and the Logical/Mathematical intelligence with the list.

159

Triangular Teaching

Engaging the Scripture

Divide your class into four teams. Assign each team one of the Gospel accounts of the empty tomb: Matthew 28:1-8; Mark 16:1-8; Luke 24:1-12; John 20:1-10. Provide each participant with a copy of the Empty Tomb worksheet in the Appendix. Invoke 33 seconds of silence prior to and following the reading of Scripture aloud. Invite each team to read their assigned Gospel account of the Resurrection silently. Then ask one person from each group to read the Scripture aloud within their own group. Ask that the remaining members of each group listen with their whole beings.

Explain that those who regularly attend worship on Easter Sunday have heard each of the Gospel accounts. Explain that with this reading, you are going to listen with both hemispheres of your brain and focus on gaining a "whole-brained" experience of the Easter story. Explain that while technically we know that each hemisphere of the brain is involved in complete learning, for many years we have considered the left brain to house the cognitive, semantic, and rational aspects of learning and the right brain to house the poetic, musical, and creativity-based aspects of learning. Ask for the Scriptures to be read aloud again in each group. This time participants are to listen for and record specific data that is "Left-Brained Information" (head learning) and "Right-Brained Formation" (faith learning). Allow four minutes and 12 seconds for this activity.

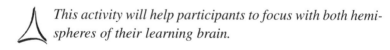 *This activity will help participants to focus with both hemispheres of their learning brain.*

Give each group a sheet of newsprint with the labels LEFT BRAIN and RIGHT BRAIN. When the allotted time is up, ask each group to discuss their individual worksheets and create a group worksheet, which will be presented to the entire class. Ask that as they discuss their personal sheets, when they agree on information-based items, to record them on the LEFT BRAIN side of their newsprint. When they agree on information that is faith-based, they are to record these items on the RIGHT BRAIN side of their newsprint. Allow seven minutes and seven seconds for this task. When the allotted time is up, invite each group to share their newsprint with the total class.

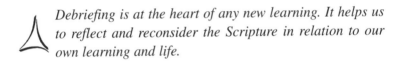 *This activity continues the process of focusing on both hemispheres of the learning brain and paying attention to what we know and what we believe through faith. This whole-brained approach engages both critical and creative thinking. The lists engage Logical/Mathematical intelligence. Discussion engages Interpersonal intelligence.*

Debrief this activity by asking for insights into the Easter Scriptures based on focusing on both left and right hemispheres in learning.

Debriefing is at the heart of any new learning. It helps us to reflect and reconsider the Scripture in relation to our own learning and life.

Life Application

Invite participants to retrieve the stone that they received when they entered the classroom. Explain that they are going to make a metaphorical connection to the stone that was rolled away from the entrance to the tomb for new life to emerge. Ask participants to consider what stones need to be "rolled away" in their lives so that new life in Christ might emerge. Assure participants that this will be a private activity between them and God. There will be no need to share their stone stories. Ask participants to consider what actions they might need to take to roll the stone away and how they might engage in those action steps. Invite participants to write a word or a symbol on their stone to capture their thoughts.

Triangular Teaching

Allow for three minutes and 37 seconds of reflection and writing (if they choose to write).

Creative and critical thinking are employed here as participants use the powerful tool of metaphor to examine their lives in relation to the Easter Scripture. Verbal/Linguistic, Logical/Mathematical, Bodily/Kinesthetic, Naturalist, and Intrapersonal intelligences are called into play for this activity.

For Personal Reflection
Invite participants to record in their journals any insights and perhaps some actions that need to be taken that have come out of this lesson on the empty tomb. Encourage them to take their stones with them as a reminder of new life in the risen Christ.

Closing Prayer
Close by singing or reading a favorite Easter hymn and asking God to help us as we venture into a new life in the risen Christ.

Leader Reflection

Where did you notice "aha's" during this lesson?

Which activities prompted the most participant involvement?

How/where might you "tweak" this lesson according to the needs of your class?

How did you grow as a teacher/learner through this lesson?

Checking the Triangle

Look at the triangle below. In the space near the multiple intelligences side, write the ways of learning demonstrated in each of the activities. In the space near the critical and creative thinking side, write which thinking process is supported by each of the activities. Consider whether an activity will be listed on more than one side of the triangle. Write any other ideas for activities that occur to you near the appropriate sides of the triangle.

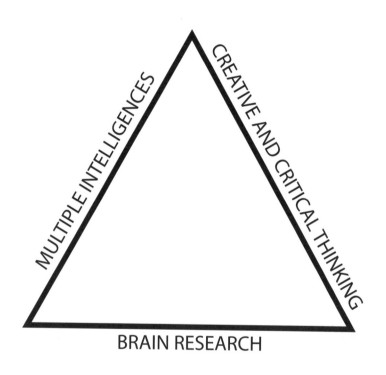

MULTIPLE INTELLIGENCES

CREATIVE AND CRITICAL THINKING

BRAIN RESEARCH

Doubting Thomas

Scripture: John 20:24-29

Materials Needed:
- Bibles
- Newsprint/markers
- Copies of the Personal Belief Inventory (Appendix, page 185)
- Bible verses written on newsprint or whiteboard, as described in "Life Application"
- Timing device
- Journals

Pre-teaching Strategy

Explain that so much in our world today is fraudulent. Advertising campaigns claim wonderfully slimming things will happen to your waistline if you just pop this pill or drink this shake. Internet ads bombard us with offers too good to be true. People show up at your door or on your Internet connection claiming to be who they are not. Invite participants to select a partner and answer the question, "What does it take to make you believe something?" Allow one minute and 47 seconds for discussion. At the end of the allotted time, invite responses to be shared with the total group. Explain that today we are going to learn that doubting is nothing new. It is a human trait to be doubtful, and people were exhibiting this trait in Jesus' time—in fact, one of Jesus' own chosen disciples had doubts about Jesus' resurrection and appearance before the disciples.

This activity uses Interpersonal intelligence to explore doubting as a human trait. The discussion provides a way for participants to connect to their lives the story of Thomas in John 20:24-29.

Engaging the Scripture

Invite participants to read John 20:24-29 silently. Invoke 33 seconds of silence. Invite a volunteer to read this Scripture aloud. Again, invoke 33 seconds of silence to allow participants to examine their hearts. Ask participants to consider this question in their heart only (no need for a show of hands), "How many of you can identify with Thomas?"

A true story from the author: A teacher was working with about 30 third and fourth grade children. She was talking about the post-Easter story of Jesus' resurrection and his appearing to the disciples. A fourth grade boy raised his hand and said, "I don't believe that—you know all that stuff about Jesus dying and coming back to life."

Ask participants what they would have done were they in this teacher's place. Invite responses.

Explain that the teacher took a deep breath as all the rest of the children were watching closely for her reply and said, "I don't understand it. I just know it happened. There are a lot of things I don't understand. I put a piece of paper on a fax machine yesterday, and within seconds the message appeared on a machine in Nashville, Tennessee. I don't understand that either, but I know it happened."

Explain that the answer appeased a child, but would it appease you? Ask, "What 'proof' would you need to be convinced that Jesus rose from the dead and returned to talk with his disciples?" Invite responses.

 Sharing a true story, inviting responses, and inviting participants to think this problem through will create an

atmosphere of introspection and careful consideration of their reasoning. Assuring participants that they need not respond out loud will ease any sense of stress that might present itself. This activity calls upon both Intrapersonal and Interpersonal intelligences and invites critical thinking about the Resurrection.

Ask participants to fill out their copy of the Personal Belief Inventory in the Appendix. Assure participants there are no wrong answers as this is a personal inventory and they will only share what they deem comfortable.

Allow five minutes and 37 seconds to complete this task. As they complete this task, invite participants to find a partner and share their answers. Be sure to remind them that they will share only what is comfortable. Those who do not wish to share may remain silent and contemplative.

This exercise calls upon both Interpersonal and Intrapersonal intelligences to help participants explore belief. Listing engages Logical/Mathematical intelligence and critical thinking.

Life Application
Direct participants to the newsprint, on which are written Bible verses concerning doubt and belief. Invite participants to form five groups and consider one of the following:

• Mark 9:24: "I believe; help my unbelief."
• John 20:29b: "Blessed are those who have not seen and yet have come to believe."
• Mark 1:15: "The time is fulfilled, and the kingdom of God has come near; repent, and believe in the good news."
• Mark 11:23: "Truly I tell you, if you say to this mountain, 'Be taken up and thrown into the sea,' and if you do not doubt in your

heart, but believe that what you say will come to pass, it will be done for you."

• Mark 11:24: "So I tell you, whatever you ask for in prayer, believe that you have received it, and it will be yours."

Invite each group to consider their quotation and discuss it in their group for three minutes and 48 seconds. At the end of the allotted time, ask a representative from each group to respond to the total class with insights from their quotation and small group discussion.

Suggest that there are times when we are faced with something that defies critical thinking, scriptural accounts, reason, tradition, or experience. When all else fails—trust your faith! Thomas had an advantage—he was invited to see and touch. We do not have that advantage, sometimes we must depend on faith alone.

These biblical quotations provide grounds for critical thinking and faith enrichment. It is not uncommon for Christians to have doubts from time to time. Helping participants to come to grips with the fact that they are not alone imparts a sense of relief and the knowledge that we can have doubts and still believe—a very comforting place to be. The activity engages Interpersonal intelligence and critical thinking.

For Personal Reflection
Invite participants to record in their journals anything that struck a chord concerning doubt and belief in the story of Thomas.

Closing Prayer
Close with a prayer for acknowledging our doubts and the fact that we are not alone. We ask for faith to sustain us in times of doubt.

Leader Reflection

Where did you notice "aha's" during this lesson?

Which activities prompted the most participant involvement?

How/where might you "tweak" this lesson according to the needs of your class?

How did you grow as a teacher/learner through this lesson?

Checking the Triangle

Look at the triangle below. In the space near the multiple intelligences side, write the ways of learning demonstrated in each of the activities. In the space near the critical and creative thinking side, write which thinking process is supported by each of the activities. Consider whether an activity will be listed on more than one side of the triangle. Write any other ideas for activities that occur to you near the appropriate sides of the triangle.

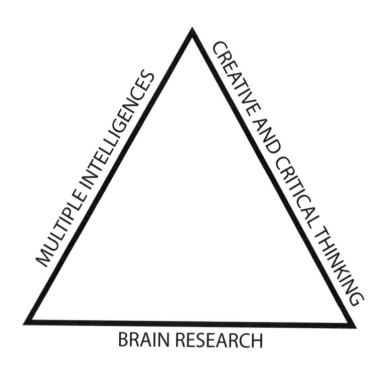

Do You Love Me?

Materials Needed:
- Bibles
- Newsprint/tape/markers
- Paper/pencils
- Timing device
- Journals

Pre-teaching Strategy

When I help my grandson go to sleep, the ritual we have established is that we read a book (or two or three) and say a prayer. I then ask him, "Who loves you?" His immediate response is, "You do." I concur and then ask him who else loves him, and we go through a litany of names. I believe this is an important exercise for children of all ages. I think we need to know that we are loved by many people. I also ask him whom he loves, and we continue our litany.

Consider your own life—who loves you? Make a mental list or write the names in your journal. It is an important human need to love and be loved. It was also a question Jesus asked Peter specifically—"Do you love me?"

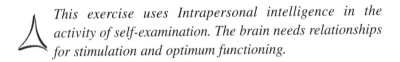

This exercise uses Intrapersonal intelligence in the activity of self-examination. The brain needs relationships for stimulation and optimum functioning.

Engaging the Scripture

The power of John's Gospel lies in metaphor. This Gospel relies heavily upon word pictures and symbolism. Consider the following story. As it is read, listen for symbolism and insights. Explain that John tells a wonderful story about Jesus appearing to the disciples and feeding them on the shore of the lake. The resurrected Jesus appeared to his disciples behind locked doors (20:19-23), spoke to Thomas (20:24-29), and prepared breakfast on the beach (21:1-24). Invoke 33 seconds of silence. Invite participants to listen to this Scripture with their entire beings. Read John 21:9-17 aloud. Invoke another 33 seconds of silence to allow Scripture to be internalized. Ask for responses and insights of what participants heard in this story.

When the Scripture has been read and responded to, form three teams. Explain that each of the following pairs of Scriptures connects. Read both sets of Scriptures and within your group decide what the connections are. Be prepared to share them with the rest of the class. Allow five minutes and 23 seconds for the groups to complete their paired Scripture study.

Ask each of the groups to read:
Team 1—John 21:9-17 and Matthew 26:30-35
Team 2—John 21:9-17 and John 10:7-16
Team 3—John 21:9-17 and Mark 14:72

When the allotted time is up, invite group members to share their observations and insights as they compared the two Scripture accounts. Debrief this exercise by asking for insights.

Verbal/Linguistic, Logical/Mathematical, Intrapersonal, and Interpersonal intelligences are called into play in this exercise. Creative and critical thinking are employed as participants need to make the connections between their two sets of Scripture.

Life Application

Invite participants to return to the list they have created of people who love them. Ask participants how they know these people love them. Ask participants to consider what is required in a loving relationship. Ask what Jesus required of Peter and how that might translate metaphorically into their own loving relationships. Ask the participants to continue their train of thought as they move beyond their immediate loved ones and extend it out to people with whom they come into contact. How might they act if Jesus had fed them and asked them to remember him; how might they act if they were asked to "feed my sheep"?

Debrief this exercise by asking for insights.

This activity calls upon Intrapersonal intelligence to help participants consider a loving relationship in a new way and hopefully take some steps to ensure a continuance of this relationship into different aspects of their lives. It engages critical and creative thinking skills.

For Personal Reflection

Invite participants to record in their journal insights gained from the exploration of love in John 21:9-17.

Invite participants to look carefully around the room and select an item. Once the item has been selected, ask participants to consider how the item chosen is like the Bible lesson. If you have chosen to teach these Bible lessons as a long-term Bible study, also ask how the item is like any of the previous lessons participants have experienced. For example, tape might be like the Scripture that holds the lessons together. A cup might express the notion of the lessons as cups that "runneth over" with information. Invite sharing as is comfortable.

Triangular Teaching

This activity is a metaphorical exercise that engages critical and creative thinking. It also engages Visual/Spatial intelligence in order to invite discussion and reflection over the connection between the objects and their experiences.

Closing Prayer
Close with a prayer of remembering whom we love and who loves us, recalling our love for and from Jesus.

Leader Reflection

Where did you notice "aha's" during this lesson?

Which activities prompted the most participant involvement?

How/where might you "tweak" this lesson according to the needs of your class?

How did you grow as a teacher/learner through this lesson?

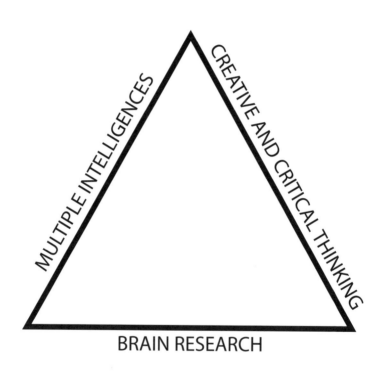

Triangular Teaching

Checking the Triangle

Look at the triangle below. In the space near the multiple intelligences side, write the ways of learning demonstrated in each of the activities. In the space near the critical and creative thinking side, write which thinking process is supported by each of the activities. Consider whether an activity will be listed on more than one side of the triangle. Write any other ideas for activities that occur to you near the appropriate sides of the triangle.

MULTIPLE INTELLIGENCES

CREATIVE AND CRITICAL THINKING

BRAIN RESEARCH

Appendix

Ways of Learning Profile

Read entirely through the following statements that relate to saying and doing. When you have read them all, go back and consider the one that primarily describes the way you function. Place a star next to that statement. Then re-read the information and find one or two other statements that relate to the way you function. Place a check mark next to your second and third choices. Please remember, we all can function in each of the different ways of learning, but we PREFER some of them over others. Your language and actions reflect ways you prefer to learn. Consider your own preferences profile as you reflect upon your language and actions.

Musical/Rhythmic
<u>Saying:</u> "It sounds like what you're saying is . . ."
<u>Doing:</u> being aware of voice inflection, tone, and rhythm of speech as well as having an interest in words and how they are used

Verbal/Linguistic
<u>Saying:</u> "Please explain what you mean by that."
<u>Doing:</u> providing detailed explanations of most things as well as requiring definitions, metaphors, word derivatives, etc. to make learning complete

Visual/Spatial
<u>Saying:</u> "I see what you mean!"
<u>Doing:</u> drawing or doodling to visualize the concept as well as using visuals (graphic organizers, maps, videos, etc.) to make learning complete

177

Triangular Teaching

Logical/Mathematical
<u>Saying</u>: "I don't quite following your reasoning."
<u>Doing</u>: outlining steps of a process in your head as well as considering the logical progression of information and organizing the facts to make learning complete

Naturalist
<u>Saying</u>: "I can think best when I take a walk outside."
<u>Doing</u>: creating metaphors based on the natural world to complete the learning process

Interpersonal
<u>Saying</u>: "I need to talk that through with you."
<u>Doing</u>: discussing ideas and learning with others as well as enjoying a team approach to complete the learning process

Intrapersonal
<u>Saying</u>: "I need some time to think about that."
<u>Doing</u>: needing time to be alone to reflect and consider options as well as liking to work alone to make learning complete

Bodily/Kinesthetic
<u>Saying</u>: "Run me through the process."
<u>Doing</u>: using body language as a means of expression as well as moving and/or manipulating objects to aid the thinking process and make learning complete

VENN Diagram

A VENN diagram is a graphic organizer used to highlight the commonalities and differences between two areas of content.

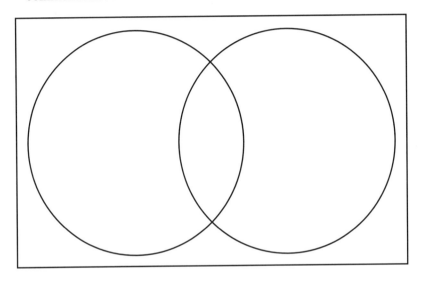

VENN Diagram Example

MATTHEW

LUKE

Joseph's Story
Magi
Dream

Birth
Angel
Bethlehem

Mary's Story
Shepherds
Elizabeth

Mind Map

A mind map, or concept map, is a visual representation of an idea and the many ideas that surround and are connected to it. One idea may lead to another.

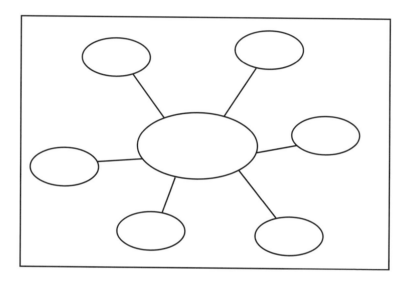

Mind Map Example

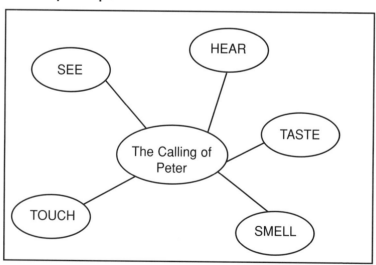

Chart of the Senses

SEE

HEAR

TASTE

TOUCH

SMELL

Open-Ended Sentences

Complete the open-ended sentences below.

I am _____

I am _____

I am _____

I am _____

I am _____

I am _____

I am _____

[Fold the page here. Give the page to a partner who will complete the open-ended sentences below and return the page to you.]

I see you as _____

I see you as _____

I see you as _____

I see you as_____

I see you as_____

I see you as_____

I see you as_____

"Who Do You Say I Am?"

Write answers in all the spaces below:

Who do you say I am? _____

Who do you say I am? _____

Who do you say I am? _____

Who do you say I am? _____

Who do you say I am? _____

Who do you say I am? _____

Empty Tomb

THE TOMB IS EMPTY—HE IS NOT HERE—HE IS RISEN

LEFT BRAIN Factual information	RIGHT BRAIN Faith-filled feelings

Personal Belief Inventory

Write responses in the spaces provided.

• Things I believe with all my heart to be true:

• Things I am pretty sure about:

• Things I have trouble believing:

• Things I believe are not true:

Permission is granted for the original purchaser to reproduce this page provided that the following acknowledgement line is included on each copy: *Triangular Teaching*, by Barbara Bruce (Abingdon, 2007).

Glossary

Analogy—a figure of speech; a comparison of two dissimilar items using the connecting words "like" or "as" (The kingdom of God is like . . .). Metaphor and simile are two kinds of analogies.

Brain Research—a rapidly growing, multidisciplinary field of study about how the brain functions in all walks of life.

Creative and Critical Thinking—dual aspects of the creativity process; both are necessary for total in-depth consideration of an idea or concept. Creative thinking refers to fluency, flexibility, elaboration, and originality. Critical thinking refers to processes of investigation, discernment, and conclusions based on gathered information.

Debrief—a powerful tool to help participants gain insights into exercises and activities by discussing their thoughts and feelings of both the content and process following a learning experience.

Disciple—the Greek word for *learner*. It refers to an apprentice or pupil who follows and/or has an allegiance to the teachings and commitment of a particular teacher.

Graphic Organizer—a visual tool with which to organize information in an orderly fashion to aid in understanding.

Improvisational Drama—"improv" is a form of drama with no script. Players are given the skeleton of an idea and then act it out as they believe it should happen. We are using a modified form of

Triangular Teaching

"improv" in which the actors are familiar with the Scripture story and act out the experience and emotions they carry with them.

Midrash—literally means to search, inquire, or interpret. Midrash is a type of biblical interpretation that builds on the information presented and creates a story based on this information that "fills in the blanks." Since we do not know the rest of the story, there are no right or wrong answers as long as the midrash maintains the biblical infrastructure.

Mind Map—a graphic organizer to help participants see the relationships between the concepts of the Scripture story. See page 180 in the Appendix.

Multiple Intelligence Theory—a theory espoused by Dr. Howard Gardner of Harvard University and his disciples concerning the many and varied ways the brain encodes information. Each person is born with at least seven different ways of acquiring and using information.

Pre-teaching Strategies—strategies to help participants move from "getting there" to "being there." These strategies help to ease participants into a lesson by using a variety of tools and techniques. While most often these strategies are used at the beginning of a lesson, they may be inserted into the lesson at any point when needed for clarification. These strategies "hook" the brain into discovery about the Scripture to be studied.

Scotoma—an area of diminished vision. Metaphorically, a mental scotoma often keeps us from understanding fully and clearly as we study Scripture.

Synoptic Gospels—the Gospels of Matthew, Mark, and Luke. These Gospels contain much of the same material.

The Visual Bible—three books of the Bible are available in this printing: Matthew, John, and Acts. Each contains only the words of Scripture (NIV) and is filmed on location in Egypt and Israel. This resource is an invaluable tool for helping participants to actually "see" the story. For example, the Sea of Galilee in the film is *really* the Sea of Galilee. (See Bibliography for reference information.)

Timing Device—a good timer with a second counter is a helpful tool. It becomes an objective measure of time, and your participants will get used to completing tasks within the time provided. Minutes and seconds are given to provide interest. This strategy peaks interest and gets people thinking about more than minutes alone.

VENN Diagram—a graphic organizer to help participants see the commonalities and differences between two areas of content. See page 179 in the Appendix.

Bibliography

Creative and Critical Thinking

The Artist's Way: A Spiritual Path to Higher Creativity, by Julia Cameron (Tarcher/Putnam, 2002).

The Creative Journal: The Art of Finding Yourself, second edition, by Lucia Capacchione, Ph.D. (New Page Books, 2001).

The Creative Spirit, by Daniel Goleman, Paul Kaufman, and Michael Ray (Plume, 1993).

More Parables From the Back Side, by J. Ellsworth Kalas (Abingdon Press, 2005).

The New Drawing on the Right Side of the Brain, by Betty Edwards (Tarcher/Putnam, 1999).

Parables From the Back Side: Bible Stories With a Twist, by J. Ellsworth Kalas (Abingdon Press, 1998).

The Storyteller's Companion to the Bible: Stories About Jesus in the Synoptic Gospels, Vol. 9, edited by Dennis E. Smith and Michael E. Williams (Abingdon Press, 2005).

The Thirteen Apostles, by J. Ellsworth Kalas (Abingdon Press, 2002).

The Visual Bible: Matthew, DVD directed by Reghardt Van Den Bergh (GNN International Corp. and Visual Bible, LLC, 2004).

Brain Research

Loving God With All Your Mind: Equipping the Community of Faith for Theological Thinking, by Thomas Hawkins (Discipleship Resources, 2006).

Our Spiritual Brain: Integrating Brain Research and Faith Development, by Barbara Bruce (Abingdon Press, 2002).

The Owner's Manual for the Brain: Everyday Applications From Mind-Brain Research, second edition, by Pierce J. Howard, Ph.D. (Bard Press, 1999).

Multiple Intelligences

Intelligence Reframed: Multiple Intelligences for the 21st Century, by Howard Gardner (Basic Books, 1999).

7 Ways of Teaching the Bible to Adults: Using Our Multiple Intelligences to Build Faith, by Barbara Bruce (Abingdon Press, 2000).

Biblical Study

The Holy Bible in several translations

Synopsis of the Four Gospels, third edition, edited by Kurt Aland (United Bible Societies, 1979).

Teaching the Bible to Adults and Youth, by Dick Murray (Abingdon Press, 1993).